DATE DUE

The Art of Killing Kudzu

Management By Encouragement

The Art of Killing Kudzu

Management By Encouragement

A Guide For Communicating Encouragement To
The Employee, The Customer/Client
And The Insecure Partner

Stephen M. Gower

Lectern Publishing
P.O. Box 1065, Toccoa, GA 30577

First edition, published 1991 by LECTERN PUBLISHING, P.O. Box 1065, Toccoa, GA 30577.

Library of Congress Catalog Card Number: 91-62281

ISBN 1-880150-50-6

Dedicated To Dad

You kept trying to teach me the supremacy of "We" over "I." And, when I flatly ignored you, you consistently and lovingly encouraged me to do better. Thanks Dad.

Acknowledgments

We do not travel alone on the road that leads to the completion of a significant project. There are people who help us prepare for the trip; others are there when we start; some will travel most of the journey with us; still others will be available to encourage us during the final lap of the trip.

I must confess that I have been the recipient of support and encouragement before, throughout and after the journey. This is not an "I" book. It is a "We" book.

I want to thank my family for their support. There is no doubt that their encouragement provided the springboard.

And once the project was launched, a host of friends made significant contributions. Julie Moore, Gordon Telford and Jon and Peggy McIntire helped provide the nuts and bolts for the production of the manuscript. I am still not sure what I appreciate the most—their expertise or their encouragement.

I would like to thank my cousin, copyright attorney and friend, John Harris, for his insight throughout the journey. I am truly the beneficiary of John's expertise and friendship.

As I approached the final lap, Polly Trexler, Lida Sims, India Stewart, Greg Pitts, Joe Moore and Bill Stratton were there for me. Together we crossed the finish line.

I have a deep sense of appreciation for all of these managers of encouragement.

The mission of *The Art Of Killing Kudzu — Management by Encouragement* is to provide the manager with a unique and highly effective guide for communicating encouragement to the employee, the customer or client and the insecure partner.

Contents

The Fiction

An Introduction

The Art Of Killing Kudzu — Management By Encouragement begins with a unique comparison between poor performance, or less than preferred responses, and Kudzu. Kudzu, that pesky, obstinate vine that chokes out more productive plants, is compared to a counter-productive attitude and negative approach that chokes out growth and increased productivity.

Management by encouragement is presented as the chemical that kills this Kudzu. Based upon the idea that "nobody can motivate you but you," management by encouragement features a critical and extremely effective distinction between motivation and encouragement.

The reader will discover that the motivation button can only be pushed from the inside. In other words, you cannot externally or superficially motivate the employee to kill Kudzu. You can, however, encourage the employee to kill Kudzu—both his own Kudzu and the resulting team Kudzu!

The encouragement manager does not focus on external or artificial motivation. The encouragement manager devotes energy and expertise towards the creation of a motivational environment. This motivational environment is created through management by encouragement.

Unfortunately, the external motivator often chooses to confront at the point of weakness. The encouragement manager builds an environment that is based on strength affirmation.

When the manager quits trying to motivate and starts encouraging, he will notice that the employee will be enabled or facilitated to push his own motivation button. Management by encouragement is a systemic and systematic approach to management that results, not in incessant on-off productivity or cyclical highs and lows, but in an environment that fosters increased productivity and effectiveness.

This book is divided into three sections: The Facts, The Formulae, and The Fiction. The book's first section, The Facts, is designed to help you understand Kudzu: what it is, where it grows and how it can be killed. The second section, The Formulae, certainly the meat of the book, analyzes the Kudzu-killing chemical — management by encouragement. Specifically, this section is structured around eight formulae. Each formula relates to a specific ingredient that contributes to the potency of this Kudzu-killing chemical. The final section, The Fiction, seeks to expose and explore two specific misconceptions that the encouragement manager must understand.

And, now its time to begin! Perhaps you've tried "external motivational" books. Now, try *The Art of Killing Kudzu!*

Quit trying to motivate and start encouraging.

Part One

The Facts

CHAPTER 1

Kudzu Is Bad Stuff

I fought Kudzu. And, Kudzu won!

The turf was a rare, rich, flat piece of land positioned at the foot of the Northeast Georgia mountains. It was midsummer. And it was hot; it was very hot. I was primed for an irritation.

Harvest time was several weeks away. The garden that simply began as a therapy for this speaker was about to yield bonus dividends of beans, squash, cucumbers and Silver Queen Corn. My excitement was intensifying. I was particularly looking forward to enjoying the corn. Remember, this was Silver Queen Corn. And Silver Queen Corn is to corn as a standing ovation is to possible responses for the speaker.

My excitement was escalating, but so was the heat. Sweat was burning my eyes; mosquitoes were stinging my ankles; the sun was scorching my back. Yes, I was ready for an aggravation.

Enter Kudzu! Kudzu became the irritation. And, there was no reluctance, or even hesitation, in its demeanor. Kudzu had cheerfully and eagerly accepted the role of "aggravator."

I started to leave this arena of heat, sweat and mosquitoes. Enough was enough! I had put up the tiller and put down the hoe. I headed up the hill; I could almost taste the cool tea waiting for me in the truck. I knew my much needed drink would be blessed with a couple of ice cubes. I could hardly wait! Halfway up the hill, I stopped. I wanted one more glance at that beautiful sight. I turned and sat on a convenient stump.

What I viewed was impressive! Had I possessed the energy, I would have puffed my chest with pride. Why, my tilling was straight! The dirt was dark where I had just plowed. It contrasted nicely with the adjacent untilled land. And, the plants were a healthy green. Everything looked great.

Wait! There was an exception. Something was wrong with the corn. It was the only section that I had not tilled this week. Compared to all the other crops, it looked crowded, almost emaciated.

I could not leave my beloved Silver Queen Corn like that. Walking back down the hill, I thought to myself, "You just cleared that section a couple weeks ago." I wondered, "Could the morning glories have come back that quickly?" I continued diagnosing the problem, "What about the Kudzu? Surely it was not back already!"

It was! The Kudzu was back already! A survey of my Silver Queen Corn patch revealed few morning glories, but "Oh, the Kudzu!" And, I had just cut it back.

The Aggravator had stretched its ugly body up the hill and into my Silver Queen Corn rows. Not only had it extended itself into the rows, it had raised its pompous head up the stalks. It was much worse than it had been just two weeks before when I thought I had "cut it back for good." The Kudzu was growing wild; and so was I.

I was too tired, too sun burned, and too badly bitten by the mosquitoes to have to fool with this stuff. But fool with it I did; and fool-like I felt. I was hot and irritated; but I would not be defeated.

Three hours, and many more mosquito bites later, I left. I had carefully unraveled Kudzu down from the corn, stalk by stalk. I had worked my way back to the bank and to the root of the problem. I had found the root of each Kudzu vine; and I had dug and dug and dug. I had sneered with victory each time I thrashed the Kudzu with my mattock. It was a feeling similar to the one I had experienced when I swatted and killed those mosquitoes. Surely this time I had removed enough of the root to kill the Kudzu — for good.

I had not! I had not killed the Kudzu—for good!

After a rather lengthy absence, I returned. It was obvious that my corn patch had received another visit from Kudzu. This time the problem did not seem quite so severe. But, there should have been no more Kudzu at all. I retrieved the mattock and whacked at the Kudzu roots for another hour. Certainly this additional punishment would prove to be the knock-out punch.

It did not. It did not prove to be the knockout punch! To make this long story of long Kudzu short, let me relate to you that I lost nearly three of my sixteen rows of Silver Queen Corn to Kudzu. This pesky, obstinate vine wore me down and won. It deprived those corn stalks the nutrients and sun and water they needed. Kudzu strangled the Silver Queen.

Management By Encouragement

Kudzu is bad stuff! It grows wild; and it chokes out the good stuff. Kudzu leaves its home and boisterously breaks into vegetable gardens.

Controlling Kudzu becomes a time consuming, and often unsuccessful, ordeal. Kudzu allows you no vacation. Unruly Kudzu is not content with being difficult to manage. Its higher desire is to overpower. The one responsible for the suffocation of the Silver Queen Corn was Kudzu!

I understand that many refer to Kudzu as a prostrate vine—meaning that Kudzu has a tendency to recline or to bend or to be humble. This is not the Kudzu I know. There's nothing humble about it.

Its tuberous roots yield a product that is arrogant and stubborn. Battling Kudzu is like scuffling with an octopus. Just when you wrestle two tentacles down, up pop six tentacles.

There was nothing reclining about the Kudzu I fought. And the only things bending were my Silver Queen Corn stalks.

Kudzu does not know how to be still. Kudzu wiggles. Kudzu grows where it wills. It invades gardens, landscapes, junkyards, roadsides and more. It takes over.

Kudzu is mighty tough; and Kudzu is arrogant!

CHAPTER 2

Kudzu Grows Here

Kudzu does not know its place!

The laboratory for the Kudzu of the first chapter of this book was my garden. The crucible for the Kudzu of the remaining chapters is a plethora of corporations, associations, industries, communities, and individuals throughout our country.

The milieu for Kudzu is not limited to roadsides, junkyards and vegetable gardens. Its environment includes as well: shopping malls, banks, radio stations, nursing homes, dentist offices, clothing stores, insurance agencies, hospitals, corporate headquarters and colleges.

The habitat for Kudzu is not merely dirt. It is concrete and asphalt. It is air and water. The setting for Kudzu is not just between trees. It is behind walls and between desks. It is in offices and cars and planes and boats.

The ultimate scene for Kudzu is not where it nestles itself around fence posts or road signs or vegetables. Kudzu's utmost and most comfortable habitat is between people and in the mind!

The surroundings for Kudzu are not limited to turf and trees and telephone poles. Its environment also includes: teams, departments; employers, employees; customer service representatives, customers; teachers, students; pastors and missionaries, members; supervisors, supervisees; professionals, clients and patients; executives, subordinates; coaches, players; and moms and dads and their young ones and their old ones.

Kudzu thrives not only in the environment of a rich soil. It also blossoms in the cupboard of the frustrated and discouraged mind!

Kudzu does not know its place. It does not know where it belongs. It will depart the hill and enter the vegetable garden.

Moreover, Kudzu will not even stick to the definition that we have applied to it for ages. It will roam from the literal vine to the awesome analogy that suggests that what happened in my garden can happen at work, school and home!

Management By Encouragement

Kudzu, unfortunately, is much more than an obstinate, pesky vine extending from robust tuberous roots. Kudzu is a counter-productive attitude and a cantankerous, negative approach that intensifies rapidly and chokes out growth and increased productivity.

This Kudzu sprouts from the seeds of ambiguity, frustration, disappointment, and discouragement. Its growth is fertilized by indifference, ineffective communication and avoidance. The ah-hah button is seldom pressed. The uh-oh button is overworked. Kudzu grows here!

Kudzu grows wild: from receptionist to secretary to employer, from department head to branch manager to executive vice president, from agency to agency, and from employer to employee. Kudzu's frenzied expansion is both vertical and horizontal. Superiors and subordinates are affected; peers are impacted as well. Kudzu invades teams, staffs, departments and management.

Track this Kudzu with radar and you will observe the awesome speed at which it can accelerate. The scary phenomenon is that Kudzu does not merely change lanes; it adds lanes. It plays havoc on different tracks at the same time.

When Kudzu decides to move laterally, its point of origin is not weakened; that starting place is strengthened. When Kudzu moves up or down the ladder, the particular rung on the ladder where Kudzu initially took root is not loosened; it is reinforced!

One bank teller impacted by Kudzu is no less injured simply because Kudzu has attacked another bank teller. To the contrary, Kudzu's venom has a cumulative and cyclical effect on both bank tellers.

The program department of a radio station has no reason to rejoice when Kudzu expands from programming to sales. To the contrary, there is serious cause for concern. As Kudzu grows wild, it seeks to crush larger and larger chunks of the organizational pie.

Last year a terrible tornado hit our city. I was in an Atlanta mall when I first heard about it. The ride home seemed much longer than normal. I could not believe the destruction. Both rural and suburban communities had been struck. The twister began in the county and marched toward town.

The fact that this ball of wind damaged the town also did not in any way make our county residents hurt less! The spreading of damage does not lessen the original hurt. Kudzu grows wild: in counties, in cities, between people! Kudzu's growth both intensifies and expands the initial hurt.

Management By Encouragement

We must remember that Kudzu not only grows wild between people, it also thrives boisterously within the mind. In this innerlife cupboard, Kudzu matures.

And as Kudzu grows stronger here, in the mind, it becomes much more confident and assertive. Kudzu does not rest until it has grown so that it can affect our rest, our work, our play, our memory, our patience and our creativity! Kudzu grows wild in the mind!

Not only does this Kudzu of a counter-productive attitude and pesky, negative approach grow wild; this breed of Kudzu also chokes out the good stuff!

If the Kudzu of the first chapter deprived my Silver Queen Corn of nutrients, sun and water, the Kudzu of the remaining chapters denies its victims the food they so desperately need.

Remember, here Kudzu's victims are not roadsides, junkyards and vegetable gardens. This Kudzu targets businesses, schools, associations, professionals, industries, communities and individuals. Accordingly, the essential food these various targets are denied may not always be the same.

Kudzu Chokes Out Profits!

In many cases, Kudzu will deny its prey profits. Kudzu chokes out profits. It attacks the attitude, affects productivity, eventually robs from profits!

Several years ago, a large food products firm called me. They had a bad case of Kudzu. One important segment of their sales force had been told that their sales territory would be reduced by a very significant amount. No immediate ointment was offered to soothe this serious hurt to the salesmen.

Adrenaline was down, anxiety was up! Both attitude and productivity had been badly wounded.

This company recognized that, since Kudzu had already affected attitude and productivity, profits could well be next. They correctly perceived that Kudzu chokes out profits.

And, Kudzu chokes out confidence. Kudzu gnaws at self-reliance. "I did badly" becomes "I am bad." Boldness disappears; hesitation increases!

Yes, Kudzu Chokes Out Confidence

The pilot indicated we were almost ready to land.

"Surely, we cannot be landing soon," I thought.

"It looks as if we are right in the middle of a mountain range."

The pilot was correct. We did land soon. And soon, I would learn that I was not the only one surprised that we would be landing "in the middle of that mountain range."

Landing at that particular airport has given more than one person a "confidence-shaking." Simply worded, the airport is perched, or positioned, in peculiar fashion in relationship to the landscape. It is arranged in such a manner as to allow perception to differ from reality. It was not like it looked.

The landing was perfect. But, it did look most unusual as we were headed toward our "final" destination.

Land in a patch of Kudzu; watch a "confidence-shaking" take place!

The Kudzu that staggers confidence has several favorite targets. The state association responsible for flying me into that most unusual airport had asked me to address two such targets—public speaking and planning and conducting meetings. Here Kudzu looks very much like nervous energy—nervous energy that is ineffectively channeled.

There are other destinations for the Kudzu that causes confidence to tremble. This Kudzu clings to the sales person and manifests itself in the form of reluctance: reluctance to call, to sell, to risk "the no."

This Kudzu attaches itself to the student and reveals itself in the form of futility: "It's useless; I can't handle this much material; I'll never learn it all."

This Kudzu clings to the employee and expresses itself in a plethora of ways: irritability, withdrawal, discouragement, absenteeism, gossip, apathy, an uncooperative spirit, many negative comments and ultimately resignation.

This Kudzu connects to the leader and declares its presence in a sinister series of inappropriate and ineffective responses. Many of these confidence-shaking responses are precipitated by the loneliness of leadership itself.

This Kudzu fastens itself to the customer and communicates in terms of disloyalty, "no-repeat" business, and again, gossip or bad press! Kudzu spreads from a dissatisfied customer to potential customers. When the customer loses confidence in the product, he becomes a tattletale. When the customer loses confidence in the service, before, after and during the sale, he tells all!

Yes, Kudzu chokes out profits and confidence; it also strangles away growth in relationships! Trust is replaced by suspicion. A cacophony of disharmony rings over the team. The diversity becomes highlighted; the unity is basically ignored.

Yes, Kudzu Chokes Out Growth In Relationships!

I was speaking for a state human services agency in another area. Fifteen minutes into the seminar, I sensed how Kudzu had rocked relationships for that particular group of people. I had been forewarned that an attitude of frustration had permeated the staff. The workers felt drained, spent, misunderstood and taken for granted.

On that day, some of the staff would hardly look at each other. The first break produced tight and closed clusters of people; some groups turned to an artificially formal or stilted behavior; and some participants literally went to a corner and continued pouting alone. They had found their convenient "pity pot place." Kudzu had won!

When Kudzu impacts potential growth in relationships, it affects the capacity of the team players to focus on team building. The members of the staff, department, crew or agency are encouraged by Kudzu to focus on those qualities that fracture and eventually erode any commonality. Team destruction becomes a hidden goal. Kudzu tears people apart.

Kudzu Chokes Out Creativity!

In addition to smothering profits, confidence and growth in team relationships, Kudzu also stifles creativity.

Adrenaline is not easily activated; those affected are not only not alert, they "don't seem to care." There's no drive to discover new ideas, no force to fashion new concepts, no effort to express or produce new designs or approaches.

Kudzu drains one's creative juices; fatigue sets in. There's not enough energy left to bring something into being! Kudzu chokes out creativity.

Don't Go Cruising With Kudzu!

If you can help it, and you can, you will not want to go cruising with Kudzu!

Several times recently, I have been asked to speak to high school and college students. My adrenaline is normally activated the moment I am even asked to speak to these young people. You can imagine how excited I become once I actually start speaking to them.

Management By Encouragement

I remember, in particular, one conference that involved students from up and down the Eastern Seaboard of the United States. We were to meet together for three days. I had been looking forward to this particular conference for a long time.

The three days meant much more to me than I had imagined. These college students were a special lot and they probably encouraged me more than I did them.

I especially appreciated their capacity to relax. They had not yet outgrown cruising—that aimless driving around for hours. And they, like most young people, would suggest that cruising was not aimless at all; cruising built relationships.

And, as I think about them now, I wonder: "Are they cruising now? And, whom are they cruising with now?"

Choose your cruising partners wisely. Don't choose Kudzu. Kudzu pilfers profits, shakes confidence, rattles relationships and causes creative urges to go down hill.

Remember, Kudzu is bad stuff; it grows wild; and it chokes out the good stuff.

Don't go cruising with Kudzu. Throw it out of the car!

CHAPTER 3

Kudzu Can Be Killed

ow do you kill Kudzu? You discover the Kudzu-killing chemical!

A group at Merck Chemical Company had invited me to speak. The advance information indicated to the employees that I would be speaking on the topic "The Art of Killing Kudzu." They were told that I had discovered a chemical that will kill Kudzu.

Were they in for a surprise! And, would I have fun!

They expected a literal chemical. Considering their work, that was a very natural expectation. It was normal for them to expect the Kudzu-killing chemical to be a real chemical. But, in a literal sense, the Kudzu-killing chemical is not a real chemical.

There is something else that the Kudzu-killing chemical is not. And, this initially surprises many. The Kudzu-killing chemical is not "motivation."

I have ceased counting the times people call and ask me to give a "motivational" speech. However, when they use the term "motivational," I assume they have not heard me before, and this is not a firm or association inviting me back for another presentation. Accordingly, I try to be understanding. However, had they heard me before, they, hopefully, would not have referred to me as a "motivational" speaker.

It is not that I resent that term. I know the person using it is being very complimentary. Indeed, I have several associates in the speaking and training industry who consider themselves motivational speakers. They also consider me a motivational speaker.

However, I resist the term "motivational" for a reason that is central to the writing of this book. I think there is a significant difference between motivation and the Kudzu-killing chemical.

The Motivation Button Is On The Inside!

I hate those things! Most airports in the country have them. They are buttons that are somehow affixed to the water faucets in the restrooms at the airport. With the palm of your hand, you mash or press them and out comes water. One press, and the water automatically gushes out.

The problem, however, is serious. The water automatically stops. What has immediately gushed out now has immediately stopped. You've got to be a whole lot faster than a middle-aged boy from Northeast Georgia if you are going to soap up and wash and rinse your hands before the water stops running down!

I have tried it every way imaginable. I have attempted to solve the problem by incessantly holding one hand on the button. But that presents another problem. Try getting soap out of a dispenser with one hand. Again, you have to push a button. And, with many dispensers, it is almost impossible to push the button and catch the dripping soap with one hand. Fortunate is the man or woman with very long fingers. But, even then it is a very difficult task.

Perhaps the only good thing about those aggravating contraptions, in addition to the fact that they allow no wasted water, is that they help me explain my concern with the term "motivation."

The motivation button is not located on the outside. Unlike that mechanical device on top of the faucet, the motivation button is not external in nature. It does not dangle on the outside of the human body.

The problem, however, is this: many of us operate as if true motivation is limited to that which is only controlled by an external gadget. Unfortunately, when we view motivation in this manner, we set ourselves up for a series of problems. We import a motivational speaker, or hire a motivational leader. We get a quick turn-on, the water starts flowing. Regrettably, however, we also get a quick turn-off!

Your motivation button is located on the inside; so is mine. Our motivation buttons are not positioned such that other people can push them.

But, don't we wish they were? Don't we wish that everybody's motivation button was located on the outside of their body, perhaps on their left shoulder? Don't we wish we could just push that button and they would do the work, they would clean the room, they would finish the homework, they would sell the merchandise? Don't we wish they would do exactly what we wanted, when we wanted it, in the way we wanted it?

And, what about those people whose motivation buttons we wish we could be pushing? Don't you imagine they wish that our motivation buttons were externally located? And don't you imagine that they wish they could push our buttons and we would quit bugging them and we would let them make their own choices?

Remember, the motivation button is not an external device located on the outside; it is an internal device located on the inside.

Now, I must state that there is an exception to this theory. It is my personal conviction that the exception here is The Holy Spirit. I believe that The Holy Spirit motivates; but even here, we are speaking of an in-dwelling.

Yes, the motivation button is on the inside. You cannot ultimately push another person's motivation button. If Kudzu is all over your place, your company, your team, your sales force, your management staff, your employees, your customers, you will need the Kudzu-killing chemical! It is not motivation!

Do not forget the annoying, automatic on-off button on the sink at the airport. Just when you think the water is running, it stops! Limit your arsenal to motivation; and just when you think the problem has been solved, it will resurface. External motivation does not get to the Kudzu root of the problem.

To the contrary, artificial or external motivation will actually aggravate the problem.

An Awesome Aggravation!

It was insane, almost unbelievable! But, I was seeing it with my own eyes.

I had flown out early, since a Saturday flight would save the association on airfare expenses. Sunday was a free day; the keynote was not scheduled until Monday morning.

I had a whole day to kill and spent most of the afternoon jogging on a delightful multi-mile track that allowed me to enjoy much of the Sioux Falls, South Dakota scenery. Upon returning to the motel room, I turned on the television and thought I would rest while watching the U. S. Open tennis finals.

That's when I saw it. Something almost obscene was happening. A man was serving a tennis ball at a speed that seemed to exceed one hundred miles per hour. And, that tennis ball was going exactly where he wanted it to go.

It made me sick. My serves hardly ever go where I want them to go. In a tennis match, it is not unusual for me to miss most of my first serves.

And, after I miss that first serve, I react in a fashion of anger that aggravates the situation. I take no time to regroup. In frustration and in a hurried state, I immediately attempt the second serve; and, I immediately miss again!

Management By Encouragement

The tennis world has a term that has become very descriptive for me. That term is "double fault."

Double fault is used to describe the consequences of two consecutive missed serves. Usually, my double fault experience is a direct result of an inappropriate response to the first missed serve.

Unfortunately, when we encounter initial trouble in relationship to our team members, we hurriedly and inappropriately respond with a second missed serve. Almost in knee-jerk fashion, we attempt external or superficial motivation. We aggravate the situation; we double fault!

Our people don't want us messing with their buttons. Deep down, they rebel against manipulation. What they will appreciate, however, is an environment of encouragement that will facilitate a process that enables them to push their own motivation buttons.

Do not double fault. Encourage!

Management by Encouragement Works!

If the literal Kudzu-killing chemical does not exist; and, if motivation is little more than a very temporary and possibly problematic quick-fix, then there is an actual systemic, systematic and effective approach that will kill Kudzu. The Kudzu-killing chemical is management by encouragement, and it works!

We give up trying to motivate other people. Through management by encouragement, we create a motivational environment. This environment sets the stage for employees, leaders, students, team members! They are encouraged to push their own motivation buttons.

Management by encouragement establishes a habitat that facilitates the process. Management by encouragement builds a platform that enables self-motivation. It becomes a springboard for the launching of self-actualization.

A program of management by encouragement offers an effective, systemic and systematic approach. It does not deliver a bandage. It does not present a quick-fix.

Kudzu is bad stuff; encouragement is good stuff. Management by encouragement kills Kudzu!

CHAPTER 4

Encouragement Is Good Stuff

"Have you tried a Kudzu quiche?"

The young lady was very polite. However, I was jarred somewhat when she suggested that one could actually eat Kudzu.

In my more serious and objective moments, I recognize that Kudzu may have an occasional, redeeming, legitimate purpose. Quite honestly, I don't focus in that direction much because it contrasts with the analogy I have been developing and presenting for many years.

But, eat Kudzu? I could not imagine that!

But, there it was in the envelope. It was a recipe for Kudzu quiche! Just days before, I had spoken for a Chamber of Commerce function in her city. The young lady was kind enough to write a very supportive letter of affirmation for the presentation. And, she was bold enough to include that recipe for Kudzu quiche!

I understand that a quiche is a pie-like dish. It usually involves a pastry shell that is normally filled with an unsweetened custard. Normally, that custard is blessed with several ingredients, ranging from vegetables to shrimp to cheese to bacon to ham. And, presumably, the chef can allow his or her imagination to run wild, and hence permit even the inclusion of Kudzu.

For the purposes of this book, or for almost any other imaginable reason, I am not interested in the ingredients that contribute to the ultimate quiche. But, I am very intrigued by the ingredients that eventually culminate into that which I simply call "encouragement."

Encouragement's Ingredients!

I am constantly reminding my students that presenting a quality speech is very similar to baking a cake. You provide the ingredients; you appropriately combine them; you bake the cake; and, then you deliver the cake.

Management By Encouragement

Now I am repeatedly suggesting to these young academicians that it is not enough to bake a great, delicious cake. If you do not deliver the cake effectively, your audience will never taste its deliciousness.

The subject of the delivery of the speech-cake will rise again near the conclusion of this book. I mention it here to relate the idea that, even before we become concerned with delivering the presentation, we must be sure that we have started with the right ingredients.

Accordingly, before we seek to particularize applications of the Kudzu–killing chemical, we must not only identify the ingredients; we must seek to understand them. Ambiguity will result in limited and ineffective use of this potentially powerful chemical.

Clarity, however, as it relates to a comprehension of the ingredients in encouragement, can yield maximum effectiveness when applying management by encouragement. The person who seeks to manage by encouragement must understand encouragement's personality traits. To communicate management by encouragement, one must comprehend how it works.

Break down encouragement into its simplest ingredients. Count them. You will notice eight components.

Let us begin with element number one.

Part Two

The Formulae

CHAPTER 5

Assumption Minus Articulation Equals Aggravation

A hoot minus a hooter equals hootlessness!

I noticed it just as I was pulling into the motel. Little did I anticipate that it would become a centerpiece for the next morning's presentation.

I was in the county to address a large group of educators. They were about to embark on a new, challenging year. I arrived the evening before because the affair was a breakfast event. It was dark.

And, that lighted billboard really caught my eye. It was simple. There was a large owl to the right; to the left was the phrase "we give a hoot;" underneath was the name of the advertiser.

There are several reasons why that particular

billboard caught my attention. It was bright and colorful; and, it featured one of my favorite birds.

I am especially intrigued by the owl's hoot. I understand that some owls can hoot in such a powerful way that the sound of their hoot can be heard from quite a distance.

But, when that billboard said "we give a hoot," it was not saying "we emit a powerful sound like the owl."

It was affirming no utterance at all. It had nothing to do with the owl's vocal chords. That billboard referred not to a fine resonance, but to an opinion. It had nothing to do with amplification; it had to do with an attitude!

In our culture, when we say "we give a hoot," we are not referring to a noise; we are suggesting a particular feeling, expressing a concern. We are saying "we care."

There is a tremendous and an exceptionally important difference between the hoot we feel, and the hoot the wise owl utters. The former is passive; the latter is active. The first is not heard; the second is heard.

The "hoot" we sense may be insular in nature. We may feel this hoot in isolation. Someone could be right beside us and not even be aware that we are "giving a hoot." However, if you are standing adjacent to an owl when he hoots, you will know it.

The disparity between the hoot that is a concept and the hoot that is an expression must be comprehended by the manager who desires to communicate encouragement. To understand this is to comprehend ingredient number one!

Do not fail to recognize the difference between the hoot we feel and the hoot the owl hoots! If you deny this distinction, you will not be able to kill Kudzu!

The owl does not merely "give a hoot;" he hoots! In the case of the owl, he who hoots is a hooter! Remember, a hoot minus a hooter equals hootlessness! And, hootlessness must become a stranger to the one who seeks to kill Kudzu through management by encouragement.

Assumption Without Articulation

The first ingredient in management by encouragement is: awareness of the tendency to communicate through current of consciousness. Its reminder formula is: *assumption minus articulation equals aggravation.*

I often refer to this same phenomenon as

stream of consciousness. However, many are inclined to confuse that with a literary term by the same name. The truth is, however, that current of consciousness, or stream of consciousness, or avenue of assumption will "do in" the one who seeks to do management by encouragement.

Awareness of this toxin is important to the encourager! That explains why it has the primacy of being referred to as ingredient number one in the Kudzu–killing chemical.

Be aware of this poison. Do not forget that the tendency toward current of consciousness, or stream of consciousness, is a venom. It destroys effective communication!

By definition, current of consciousness is described as the assumption, or presupposition, that someone knows what we know.

We mistakenly theorize that someone knows that "we give a hoot." The truth is this: people do not respond to our "giving a hoot," people respond to our hoot, to our hooting, to the hooter!

A hoot minus a hooter equals hootlessness; a hoot plus a hooter equals hootfulness. Similarly, a care minus a carer equals carelessness; a care plus a carer equals carefulness. We must be very careful here.

Management By Encouragement

I picked up Dr. Paul Hersey's *The Situational Leader* because of an arresting inscription on the front cover – "The Other Fifty-Nine Minutes." In this book, Dr. Hersey graphically reminds the reader that, in Dr. Hersey's words, "it is the behavior of people that impacts others, not their attitudes."

The encouragement manager must be reminded that it is the hoot that makes the impression, not the "giving the hoot." In other words, people do not respond to our "giving a hoot." They might not even comprehend the fact that we "give a hoot."

But we assume that they know that we "give a hoot." We should not assume they know what we know, what we wish they knew, or how we feel! It's the assumption on our part that throws some Kudzu into our efforts to lead, to communicate, even to encourage. We presuppose that another knows what we think about them.

They are wondering what we have on our mind when it comes to them. The disparity between our assumption that they know how we feel and their curiosity, or paranoia, presents an aggravating assortment of problems.

Often the difference between our presupposition and their inquisitiveness is awesome. We assume one thing; they are perceiving quite another.

And, it is their perception that really matters. Remember, it is not the fact that we give a hoot that matters; it is whether or not we are hooting. Our associates will not respond to our passive "giving a hoot;" they may not even know that we "give a hoot!" What they will respond to is our hooting, or our non-hooting!

Perception Against Reality

I had just completed speaking to the Independent Bankers Leadership Conference in Destin, Florida. Precious spare time awaited me. I could almost feel the sand between my toes and the sun on my back as I anticipated jogging up and down the beach. My fellowship with the sea gulls would have to wait! Someone needed to talk.

"I enjoyed your presentation," he said. "But I wonder, do people forget that we bank presidents also need encouragement?"

I had earlier shared the steps this group of bank presidents needed to take if they wanted to create a motivational environment through management by encouragement. Emphasis had been placed on encouraging others. This gentleman digested the emphasis, and seemed to appreciate it; but he needed more.

Management By Encouragement

He not only wanted to learn more about management by encouragement; he wanted encouragement. He desperately wanted more encouragement, not from me, but from his staff. He went on to suggest that he did not feel appreciated or encouraged by the people with whom he worked. He felt alone; he perceived himself as one who was taken for granted.

Our relationship did not end on that day in Destin, Florida. Months later, this same bank president invited me to speak to the staff of his bank.

Florida was no longer the scene. But, we were still in the South, and he still wanted encouragement. Remember, he had been preoccupied with the way his staff did not recognize his need for encouragement. In reality, his query had been: "Why don't they encourage me?"

I had recalled our earlier conversation and I had come to that seminar with a curiosity of my own. Naturally, during the seminar I would not refer to our previous conversation. But I would be watching for the staff's reaction to their president that day. And, during the breaks, I would seek to garner as much of their attitude about him as I could. This would not mean questions on my part during the break; it would simply necessitate listening.

What I had sensed did not differ with what I

heard. Many of these employees had a deep respect for this particular bank president, their boss. Their attitude toward him was one of sincere appreciation.

He had a tough job; they knew it. They thought he was doing well; he did not know it! He did not know that they thought he was doing well. His employees assumed he knew how they felt; he did not.

They cared; they just did not express it. They appreciated their job, their work conditions, their boss! For the most part, the tellers, the proofers, the loan officers and the vice presidents had a positive attitude about their work and their employer. Their "current of consciousness" mistake was: they assumed their boss knew their attitude; and, because of the power that assumption had over them, they failed to articulate their attitude.

Bosses don't respond to their staffs' thoughts. They probably don't even know all of their staffs' thoughts.

But the tendency of the employees at this bank was to assume that their bank president knew how much they appreciated and supported him. In reality however, he perceived them to be indifferent to his need for encouragement.

They felt like encouraging him. Perhaps, they felt it so strongly that they assumed he felt "their feelings" as well. They "gave a hoot." Because they assumed he knew they "gave a hoot" about him, they failed "to hoot."

This is an extension of the current of consciousness problem. Managers of encouragement need to be aware of their tendency to assume that someone knows what they know, or that someone knows what they wish they knew.

In other words, sometimes we wish something so strongly that we assume that our wishing makes it so. People may not know what you know; and they may not know what you wish they knew just because you wish it.

Kudzu On The Other Foot

Now, this scenario involving the banker and his staff proves to be a tremendous example of Kudzu on the other foot, or Kudzu in the eyes of the "encourager" rather than the "encouragee."

Each of us probably assumes that management by encouragement is the responsibility of the leader, not the follower. Indeed, a preponderance of my presentations focus on the tendency of the boss, teacher, owner, supervisor or department head to assume that those underneath him know his feelings of support and appreciation, when in reality the subordinates may know no such thing.

The assumption on the part of the leader or manager meshes with the intensity or paranoia of the employee or supervisee in such a fashion as to yield a negative attitude. The expression of appreciation might have been all that was needed.

But appreciation stopped at the point of attitude. The feeling never reached the point of expression. Kudzu grew in the minds of the employees.

Here, however, Kudzu was thriving in the mind of this bank president, this manager. He felt lonely and discouraged; and he was at the top!

Again, the employees felt appreciation. Their error was the fact that they did not articulate or verbalize their attitude of appreciation and encouragement. They forgot, or never recognized, that there is a difference between having a feeling (giving a hoot) and behaving like a hooter (hooting).

An Aggravating Assortment of Assumptions

The encouragement manager must be aware of the harm that current of consciousness presents to all involved: the president, the staff; the professional, the client or patient; the supervisor, the supervisee; the teacher, the student; the seller, the customer; and the employee and the fellow employee.

Earlier, we suggested that the disparity between the assumption on the part of the manager and the curiosity, insecurity or even paranoia of the subordinate, presents an aggravating assortment of problems. When the assumption, "I care, and you know I care, even though I don't say I care," mingles with the insecurity expressed in an incessant "I wonder if you care," Kudzu is birthed!

The manager assumes the subordinate understood; the subordinate feels taken for granted. One is comfortable in the assumption; the other feels very ill at ease. The manager holds the idea that the one being managed understands the thoughts of the manager. The one being managed feels misunderstood and taken for granted. He does not only not know what the manager is thinking about him; he is perhaps doing some assuming himself.

No News May Be Bad News

"No news" is not always "good news!"

When the insecure employee hears no news from the employer, he wonders: "What is the boss thinking about me? Is he even thinking about me?"

It is very important to point out here that the insecure employee, and most of them are insecure, assumes the worse. He assumes that the employer is either thinking the worst possible thing he could be thinking about him, or the employer is not even thinking of him at all.

This is where some serious problems develop. It is my experience that when the manager does not act out his attitude or assumption of appreciation, the insecure subordinates, and their number is legion, do act out their attitude of feeling ignored or taken for granted.

It's an interesting, but very dangerous, cycle. It does not just take place between employer and employee. It occurs between department heads and subordinates. It appears between retailers and customers. In fact, it occurs in many settings.

A very positive attitude exists, but is not expressed; it is not acted out. And, as a result of this non-expression, there is created a correlating, negative attitude that is acted out, or expressed!

The Discouragement Cycle Begins

What we have here are partners in the crime of ineffective communication! One partner, perhaps the manager, is assuming that another partner knows what he knows. The manager gives a hoot, assumes that the employee knows that he gives a hoot; he, however, fails to translate the "giving of a hoot" into behavior that indicates he is a hooter.

In other words, this partner never acts out his appreciation. The other partner, the insecure partner, knows that he has heard nothing, seen nothing.

This insecure partner assumes the worst. He says, "He not only doesn't think much about me; he doesn't even think about me much."

And, at this point, this uneasy partner begins to form a negative attitude of his own—a negative attitude of Kudzu. And, this attitude is acted out; it is expressed. A bad situation worsens. Yes, the discouragement cycle has been initiated. Kudzu is cranking up.

Kudzu Cannot Keep Still

Much of the chapter of this book has been written at our local library. I reached the point where I felt I would benefit from a change of scenery. I have developed quite a friendship with much of the staff at that library.

And one day, partly because of that friendship,

and partly because I was beginning to feel I may have worn out my welcome, I said to the librarian, "Would you mind if I brought some flowers for your front desk here at the library?" I continued, "There are hundreds of flowers growing in my back yard. And, I would love to share some with you."

"Sure," she said. "How'd they get in your yard?"

"I planted them," I responded. "I've been working with flowers for years."

"Why Stephen," she whimsically explained, "I've discovered a new facet in your life. And, I must admit I am surprised. I would have never imagined that you could be still long enough to plant flowers."

The manager of encouragement should not be surprised with the potency of Kudzu. Kudzu cannot and will not be still long. The Kudzu of the negative attitude resulting from the poison of current of consciousness communication drains growth and stifles any positive production.

And, unfortunately, the insecure partner will not be still with his or her negative attitude. Furthermore, the resulting acting out by the insecure partner replaces a stagnant posture with regression. Things no longer cease getting better; they begin to get worse. Because Kudzu does not stay still, it spreads rapidly and has a negative effect on everything and everyone around it. Kudzu is very debilitating!

Kudzu Steals Your Energy

I wonder if my librarian would have been as startled if I had shared with her a second hobby of mine. I refer to my interest in jogging. That interest in jogging, and the point about the debilitating nature of Kudzu, causes me to think of an instance that happened not too long ago.

It was a Sunday afternoon, it was hot; and I had about jogged myself to death. I was headed back home and noticed someone walking ahead of me. As I approached, she turned around and had something to say that jostled me.

"I thought I heard the pounding sound of approaching feet," she said.

"Well thank you," I responded. "I was not aware that there was any pounding left in me."

The person who takes jogging seriously, and knows how he feels at the end of a six kilometer race, can identify with a drained, spent, exhausted feeling. It is a feeling similar to the one that Kudzu pours out on its victims. Kudzu takes the pounding out. It beats you down. And, it makes you want to throw in the towel!

The point to remember here is that the poison of current of consciousness communication, the assumption that someone knows what you are thinking or feeling, is one of Kudzu's favorite habitats. The insecure partner in this "Kudzu of assumption" scenario makes a bad situation worse when he acts out his negative attitude.

Remember, this negative attitude was precipitated because a very positive attitude of appreciation had only been "felt" by the other partner. That partner, however, did not express his appreciation to the partner who felt so uneasy. The insecure partner had his feelings hurt. Kudzu noticed this. Refusing to stand still, Kudzu attacked the insecure partner. Kudzu wore that partner down until there was no pounding left in him.

And, remember, it all began with the perception that "he doesn't care about me at all." Granted, the manager may have felt a care; but the insecure partner did not experience the care in the behavior of a carer.

Kudzu thrives in the midst of assumption; it does not stand still at all! It seizes the opportunity to take the pounding out of the partner. It will steal energy!

It's A Matter of Perception

Michael LeBoeuf's *How To Win Customers And Keep Them For Life* includes an interesting survey on "Why customers quit." Dr. LeBoeuf shares that less than one third of those customers who quit do so for reasons related to their moving away, their friendships, the competition or the product. However, as Dr. LeBoeuf shares, "sixty-eight percent quit because of an attitude of indifference toward the customer by the owner, manager or some employee."

This survey is important because it suggests what transpires when customers perceive no attitude of difference, interest or concern on the part of the business. Furthermore, I think it is appropriate to suggest that this same perceived "attitude of indifference" is why employees, students and even managers quit.

In other words, one can interpolate from this data much about employer-employee relationships. Remember, the employer may "give a hoot," may indeed have an attitude of difference, and may well assume that the employee knows of this "giving a hoot" or attitude of difference. But it is what the employee perceives that really matters.

This Kudzu Spreads In A Hurry

Current of consciousness or stream of consciousness not only relates to the assumption that our "giving a hoot" automatically flows toward the one we appreciate. It also has reference to the presupposition that our knowledge automatically flows to another person. This latter interpretation of current of consciousness has two implications for the one who seeks to encourage, or for that fact, communicate. These implications relate to language and to product!

Many times we use very technical terms. Often we use these terms so much that they become second nature to us. Our tendency is to assume that these same terms are second nature to everybody else.

Do you recall the cardinal lesson of debate? It was "define your terms." Do not assume someone has the same knowledge of your term that you do. Assume that, and Kudzu will take advantage of you as it spreads.

Similarly, quite often we become very familiar with the virtues of our product! Product knowledge becomes second nature to us. And, we erroneously assume that product knowledge of our product is also second nature to the potential customer. Wrong!

The product does not sell itself. And if you

think the product does sell itself, Kudzu will take advantage of you here. Kudzu will spread.

If you really want to encourage your sales force, remind them: "Don't assume the potential customer knows what you know about our product! Clearly articulate our product's virtues!"

Articulate! Articulate!! Articulate!!!

Remember, whether it's the hoot you give, the language you use or the product you sell, assumption minus articulation equals aggravation. Don't just assume that someone knows that you "give a hoot!" Don't just assume that someone knows the meaning of the terms you are using. Don't just assume the customer knows how good your product is. Articulate! Articulate!! Articulate!!!

Hooter, express thyself! Speaker, elaborate on the meaning of your technical terms! Salesman, explain your product's virtues! Remember, assumption minus articulation equals aggravation! Do articulate! Do articulate!! Do articulate!!!

It's a matter of communication. And, if you do not communicate effectively, don't count on Kudzu to stay still. It will not; Kudzu will not stay still. And, Kudzu will take advantage of your failure to articulate.

THE ART OF KILLING KUDZU

Kudzu will beat your people down and will take away any pounding or any energy that they might have left.

Remember, current of consciousness is a poison. Its powerful undertow is assumption! Articulation is the only anecdote that should follow assumption. But, if you don't articulate your assumption of appreciation, you will have to endure an aggravated team!

Do not assume that someone knows what you know, what you wish they knew or how you feel! Remember, Kudzu loves "the assumer."

The unfortunate reality is this: if we are angry or upset, we will be very sure that the employee, or other partner, knows how we feel! However, when we feel appreciation, when we want to affirm at the point of strength, we will not be sure that the employee or partner knows how we feel. Unfortunately, we assume. That is sad; that is not smart!

Kudzu not only dishes out a pounding; Kudzu takes any responding pounding on our part out of us!

Kudzu is bad stuff! And, an assumption without articulation, gives Kudzu an unfair advantage!

Kudzu is normally not still long enough to give the insecure partner time to regroup. When Kudzu sees current of consciousness communication in operation, Kudzu strikes in a hurry!

CHAPTER 6

Form Minus Force Equals Farce

e have a complete arsenal of communication tools; and, we are transparent!

Every year, for the past several years, I have invited several members of the family over for Christmas dinner. And they have come.

Now, I am quite sure the only reason they come is because they know the thing is catered. And, every year, the caterer sells me too much turkey.

Accordingly, every year, I've had the same dilemma. I wonder what I should do with the left-over turkey. Invariably, I head for the cabinet by the refrigerator and pull out some form of cellophane wrap.

And, the same thing always happens; I get the wrap entangled around the wrap before I get the wrap around the turkey.

But, guess what? If I'm able to pull out a clean, unentangled sheet of that stuff, and if I hold it up, I can see through it—because it is transparent.

And, so are you!

Normally, when I am discussing transparency in a keynote or seminar, I put on my glasses and say something like this: "Yes, you are transparent! And, once I put on my glasses, I can tell whether or not you're glad to be here, or whether you'd rather be watching football, a soap opera, Tom Selleck, or Bo Derek. I can observe whether or not you are finding this meaningful. And, because I too am transparent, you can observe me. By my actions, you can tell if I mean what I say and if I am prepared."

Our whole personhood speaks! And if we want to articulate, or communicate encouragement, we need to understand that we have a complete arsenal at our disposal.

We have words, and they are important. We also have actions, and they are important.

As a matter of fact, our actions either validate or contradict our words. For example, I tell you that I have time for you, that what time it is means nothing to me; you can talk to me as long as you want to. I am supposed to be listening to you and unconcerned about the time. But, I keep looking at my watch. You get a mixed signal! I am saying one thing, doing another. My whole person is talking; and you don't like what it is saying.

People can see through us. Everything about us talks: our eyes, our smiles, our frowns, our glances away, our preoccupation with self, our touch! We can give mixed signals; or we can give a signal of integrity. We can signal that we mean what we say.

If we want to be effective encouragers, we had best understand the reality of our transparency. We had best learn how to communicate sincerity, not mixed signals, not a mere going-through-the-motion.

My Favorite Physics Lesson

I learned more about physics at a fastfood restaurant than I did at Mercer University or Emory University! I had ordered a hamburger, some french fries and a coke. The young lady at the cash register took my money, gave me the change and said, "Uh-huh, vuh-muh. Yuh-ouh nuh-buh fuh-tuh."

I asked her if she could repeat it; she could, and she did, "Uh-huh, vuh-muh. Yuh-ouh nuh-buh fuh-tuh."

Finally, I said, "Young lady I'm beginning to get the idea you are trying to talk to me! But since I don't hear well, could you run that by me one more time?"

This time, the third time, she said, "Thank you very much; you're order number forty-two."

She had no speech problem. She had an attitude and a communication problem. And, oh yes, the lesson in physics she taught me that day was this: "Form minus force equals farce."

Awareness of the reality of transparency is the second ingredient in management by encouragement. And its reminder formula is: *form minus force equals farce.*

This young lady was not aware of that reality. She did not know, nor care, that she was transparent. She had the form down; but there was not force. She had words, barely; and that was it!

In her transparency, I perceived no force, no concern. She had no interest in me. She was merely going through the motions; and I noticed it. What she said and the way she said it bothered me.

Another similar experience happened quite

recently. I had just returned to the Atlanta airport and headed home when I had to stop by the mall and get a chocolate chip cookie. Before I purchased the cookie, I purchased from another location a huge cup of fruit juice.

With this large cup of juice in hand, I approached the cookie stand. I told the gentleman behind the counter that I needed a chocolate chip cookie. As I was talking to him, I was holding my gigantic cup of fruit juice right in front of me. Anyone with any vision at all would have had to see that cup of juice.

However, after handing me my cookie, the young man actually said to me, "Would you like anything to drink with that sir?"

The young man was not paying any attention to me. He was merely going through the motion. And, I noticed it. He had the form down, but there was no force.

Look Like You Sound

I thought I was going to die!

She was driving right at 70 miles per hour. I begged, "Can you please go faster?"

She accelerated, so did those jolts of pain. Finally, we arrived at the hospital.

I had imagined there would be someone there to meet us at the emergency entrance. That was a stupid thought; we had not even called ahead. But when you are dying with a kidney stone attack, you don't think clearly.

Upon entering the emergency area, we were told that all the emergency roomlets were full. I was left in the emergency room office—a desk, a typewriter, four humongous windows, no blinds, no curtains. That's right, those windows were not blessed with blind, nor curtain, nor shade. You might say the windows were naked. The whole world could see I was having a kidney stone attack.

The on-duty doctor arrived and stated, "Mr. Gower, you are having a kidney stone attack."

"I know," I replied. "Can you please give me a shot?"

He did. A couple of minutes later I asked another question, "Can I please have another shot?"

"No," he responded, "But please undress for me."

"Undress? If I move this hand, I'll die," I moaned.

"Then, undress with one hand," he suggested.

"What do I do after I get undressed? And, do I have to take everything off? Am I going to have to just stand here?" I was full of questions, and concerns.

"No," he said as he was leaving, "I'll get you a bathrobe, but please do take everything off."

Two Unfortunate Things Happened In A Hurry

The first of two unfortunate, sequential events transpired. I was able to take everything off with one hand—everything!

The second unfortunate event then occurred. The doctor forgot to send me a bathrobe! The robe would come in about another four or five minutes; but that would not be nearly soon enough.

To aggravate the situation, a nurse was now coming down the hall; no bathrobe was in her hand. But, she was headed right for the emergency room office. I was doing everything I could do to be inconspicuous. One hand covered my kidney stone; the other hand covered!

Up to this point, I had been preoccupied with two things: I did not want to die with a kidney stone; and, I did not want to die naked in a naked emergency room office!

This nurse presented me with yet another dilemma. The nurse entered the office; I was doing all right, because basically everything was covered, so to speak. Then, we had a brief conversation.

"You are Mr. Gower, are you not?"

"Yes, Why do you ask?"

"Well, Mr. Gower, have I ever told you how much I enjoy you on the radio?"

For years, I have been giving myself a gift. On Friday nights I have been broadcasting the color commentary for football broadcasts on a one hundred thousand watt FM radio station. The signal goes throughout Northeast Georgia and into portions of the Western Carolinas. This lady had obviously heard some of those broadcasts.

"Mr. Gower, you sound so good! Again, have I ever told how much I appreciate the way you sound on the radio?"

"No," I responded, "But could you please tell me later?"

She repeated, "But you sound so good!"

So far, I was handling this extremely awkward situation rather well—until she dropped the bomb!

"Mr. Gower, before I leave, could I please shake your hand?"

Now, I am immediately presented with a major dilemma! Do I remove my right hand from the kidney stone and die physically? Or, do I remove my left hand and die socially?

This decision was not as easy as it might seem. You might imagine for a moment or two what you would do if you were put in a similar situation.

Obviously, I chose to remove my left hand. But I had a serious concern, "Was she going to be a long shaker or a short shaker?"

Unfortunately, she proved to be a very, very long shaker. She was shaking; I was shaking. Finally, she quit shaking and decided to leave. But, before leaving, she had one more comment, "Mr. Gower, you sound good; but, Mr. Gower, you don't look at all like you sound!"

Follow-Through! Remember, You Are Transparent!

Once we decide to give priority to communicating encouragement, we must not forget the importance of "looking like we sound." We are transparent!

If we don't look like we sound, our transparency emits mixed signals. If, however, we look like we sound, we send a signal of sincerity and integrity.

Now, how does one look like one sounds? For just a moment let's return to tennis and the double fault experience referred to earlier in this book. One will double fault much less if one has an effective follow-through at the point of the serve.

We must follow, or even accompany our words with actions. We must mean what we say and do what we say.

If we say that we care, we must be available. If we say that we want to talk, we must really want to talk. If we say that we want input, we must at least seriously consider that input once it is offered.

In other words, if we are communicating that we want to listen to someone but incessantly look away from them, they receive mixed signals. Or, if we say that we want to treat someone like a person but talk and act in machine-like fashion, we send a mixed signal.

You Sound Like A Machine

I was about as mad when it happened as I was the day I recognized Kudzu had finally taken over my Silver Queen Corn. I was working outside, down by the tulips, the Roseglow Barberry, and the perennials, and the dog-gone phone rang!

Many times I can make it from the flower garden into the back door between ring number three and ring number four—that is, if there is a ring number four. Normally, there is not; I pick up the phone just after ring number three; no one is on the other end, they have just hung up.

On this day, unfortunately, there was a ring number four; I picked up right after that last ring, immediately after stumping my toe on the doorstep. I was hot, hurting and breathing heavily. But I managed to answer the phone.

"Mr. Grower?," she asked.

Still gasping for air, I managed to get out, "It's Gower."

Surely, she could tell the state I was in; but she preceded with gusto. She began to read a sales pitch for an encyclopedia company.

Now, with a thumping toe, sweaty eyes and the gosh awful smell of myself, I was is no mood for an encyclopedia pitch. However, I think I could have endured it, had she just talked to me about her encyclopedias.

No, she insisted on reading her script, word by painful word—no inflection, no personality, no life, no spontaneity! And, there was no way I could endure that right then.

"Excuse me," I said.

Immediately, I received the impression that

her script did not call for an interruption on my part. She was startled; she did not know what to do. That nauseating cadence resulting from the reading of a script was replaced by a pitiful stuttering resulting from the fact that she was scriptless as far as a response to my interruption was concerned. She suffered; she wallowed in confusion.

Finally, and mercifully, I took control of the conversation. I shared a brief lecture about the virtue of addressing another as a person, rather than an object. I then concluded by saying, "Now if you'd like to talk to me, rather than just read to me, I'm ready to listen."

She then, in her own words, paraphrased the script. The transparency of her voice indicated an awkwardness and a deep frustration.

I did not buy the encyclopedias; but I did feel guilty. I did not feel guilty because I did not purchase the encyclopedias. I felt guilty because I took out my frustration with the company's procedures on one of its employees. I'm quite sure that young lady was merely doing what she had been told to do—"Read the thing!"

When we merely read something, we sound like a machine! And, we are treating the intended receiver of our message in a very non-personal fashion.

Management By Encouragement

Remember, because we are transparent, people can tell when we are merely going-through-the-motion. Because people can see through us, they can tell whether we are treating them like a person or like an object. In other words, the tone of our voice speaks!

And, so do our eyes! Yes, our eyes speak. Indeed, the eyes have it!

Our eyes give us away. They indicate our availability, our preoccupation. They communicate our interest, our apathy. They reveal our sincerity, our phoniness. Yes, our eyes reveal our transparency. Our eyes speak. And, our ears talk too!

Yes, Our Ears Talk!

As an adventurous adolescent, I particularly enjoyed playing tricks on my friends. I'd call on the phone, throw my voice and pretend to be some radio announcer.

I'd say, "If you can sing this tune, I'll send you a special prize."

And invariably, my friend would begin singing; and I would begin giggling. Then, I would be caught. The response would normally be the same, "Stephen, is that you again?"

In reality, I had not disguised my voice, nor my giggle, well!

And, similarly, many of us cannot disguise the fact that we do not listen well. In reality, most of us do not listen well at all. If you doubt this fact, give this a try.

The next time an acquaintance meets you in a mall, or downtown, they will probably ask you how you are doing. Simply respond by saying, "Lousy."

I have tried that. Quite often the person predictably responds, "Great, see you later."

When we do not listen, our ears are talking. In our transparency, it will become obvious when we are more preoccupied about what we are getting ready to say next than what the person talking to us is saying now.

How many times have you sensed another's preoccupation? They imply they are listening to you; you begin a conversation and soon you get the idea they are in another world. This tendency toward preoccupation is a deterrent to effective communication for the manager of encouragement.

Now there are several things we can do here to help ourselves. One step we can take to be sure we are listening is to use questions to verify reception of the intended message.

Just last night I caught myself asking a multitude of questions to a new acquaintance. Halfway through the conversation, I apologized: "Look, I'm sorry if I'm asking too many questions. But, I'd like to share with you why I ask questions. And, if I have overused questions, please forgive me."

This new friend was quite understanding, and listened intently while I explained my reason for asking so many questions.

"I"—Twenty-Seven Times

I told her that several years ago I noticed that far too many of my conversations had been self-centered. If I had recorded these conversations, and played them back, I would have noticed the pronoun "I" being drastically overused.

As a matter of fact, one evening, now almost a quarter of a century ago, I was speaking to a particular group. I kept noticing one person in the group apparently taking very haphazard notes. It appeared as if he were occasionally marking or checking a sheet of paper.

After finishing the presentation, I asked him what he had been doing. I think he was surprised that I had noticed that he was doing anything at all.

He seemed embarrassed, but said, "I was counting the number of times you used the word 'I' in the message."

He did not want to tell me what he had been doing; for almost twenty-five years now, I have been very glad that he did tell me what he had been doing. It is one thing to use personal anecdotes to emphasize a point; it is quite another thing to mention oneself so much that highlighting oneself becomes the emphasis.

Preoccupation with self deters effective communication. When we overemphasize what we are saying, and underemphasize what someone else is saying, our transparency is communicating a lack of interest. In other words, what our ears are doing, or not doing, is saying much.

It is my experience that the use of questions designed to encourage the other partner to talk actually has a dual purpose. Most of the time, these questions will make it much easier for the other person to express himself. This utilization of questions will also help me focus on the other person. I have found if I force myself to follow this process, I cannot at the same time be talking "most of the time."

Preoccupation with self is a hindrance to effective communication. Because we are transparent, people can tell whether or not we are preoccupied with self or with them. Because people can see through us, they can tell whether "I" or "You" reigns superior in the conversation.

Transparency Equals A Double Edged Scythe

I had just finished a presentation at the Georgia World Congress Center. The person who had invited me to speak said, "Before you leave, let me show you something."

He took me to another part of the massive hallway and pointed to a nice poster that was positioned on an easel. He had prepared that poster to help draw participants to the session, "The Art of Killing Kudzu."

Now I had always had the assumption that one would think about cutting Kudzu with a sickle, but this gentleman's poster employed language and artwork that suggested one would kill Kudzu will a scythe.

I understand that the scythe is a long and curved blade—a single-edged blade. And, if I were going to use the scythe to illustrate the sharpness of the reality of our transparency, I would have to refer to that scythe as a double-edged blade.

Transparency has two edges, two sides. We are transparent before others; others are transparent before us. It is not a one way street; it involves two lanes—each going in the opposite direction. Fail to understand this and you will fail to communicate encouragement effectively.

If you sincerely want to communicate management by encouragement, you must understand both your transparency and that insecure partner's transparency. The encouragement manager must understand both sides of this scythe — this transparency.

We have spent a considerable amount of time on the transparency of the manager; let's now address the transparency of that insecure partner.

Danger—Sensitive Feelings Here!

The insecure partner will, on many occasions, send out warning signals before the situation becomes extremely serious!

Remember, the manager has an attitude of appreciation. He does not express that attitude, but assumes the insecure partner is aware of it. The insecure partner is not only not aware of the attitude of appreciation, he is wondering why he is being taken for granted.

But, before that insecurity or apprehension reaches extreme frustration, and perhaps even resignation, there is something the manager can do. Most managers, however, don't recognize these warning signals. But, if you want to stop the progression from apprehension to extreme frustration, you must recognize these signs.

Don't forget, the insecure partner is very transparent. Observe that transparency; listen, look!

Listen! You can hear the message that trouble is brewing. This uncomfortable partner may well be asking a series of questions, all of which simply illustrate uncertainty on his part. Don't take these questions lightly. Don't ignore; don't put off! Listen and communicate an understanding of what has been said.

Look! The insecure partner acts out his frustration, not only through questions, but also through facial expressions, hyperactivity, forgetfulness, tardiness, gossip and irritability.

These warning signals are not sent through words; they are communicated through actions. The employee who feels frustrated will act out that frustration in different steps that can eventually lead toward a complete cycle of discouragement.

The one who recognizes these warning signals

early may be able to interrupt and halt this cycle of discouragement. Look for: taughtness in the eyes, unusual nervousness, daydreaming, a drop in productivity, an abrupt change in work habits and impaired work relationships.

Pay attention to the questions your people ask; pay attention to their behavior! They may be trying to tell you something through their questions and through their behavior.

Your Transparency—It Either Encourages Or It Discourages

This whole concept of transparency is a tremendous phenomenon. We have addressed its reality and its awesome power here, but will encounter transparency throughout the remaining portions of this book as well. The issue of our transparency, perhaps as much as any other issue, contributes to the reality that we, as managers, are either encouraging, or we are discouraging. In other words, we, as managers, are either fueling the encouragement cycle, or we are feeding the discouragement cycle.

We, and our people, cannot exist in a vacuum. There is no neuter land; there is no neutral territory. You are either encouraging or you are discouraging.

And, your transparency is a major contributor to the outcome.

Remember, people can see through one another; and we can see through them. That insecure partner may be trying to tell you something, even though he is not actually saying anything. Look and listen! And, then when you choose to respond, don't just talk a good game, walk a good game. Back up your words with your actions.

Don't double fault! Follow-through!!

Form minus force equals farce!

CHAPTER 7

A Manager Plus A Favorite Equals A Leak

I f you have favorites, it will leak out!

Remember, we are transparent. Our team can tell if we have favorite players. If an employer has a favored employee, it will leak out; if a department head has a "pet" subordinate, it will ooze out; if a teacher has a pampered student, the other students will know it.

If a manager is selective in the way he uses the Kudzu–killing chemical, it will become apparent to the team members. If you think you can encourage one employee without encouraging other employees, you are right. But, if you think you can selectively encourage some employees without other employees knowing it, you are wrong. You are fooling yourself. It will leak out. And, the leak will lead to a flood of problems for the team! *Awareness of the ethics in encouragement represents encouragement's third ingredient.* Its reminder formula is: *a manager plus a favorite equals a leak.*

I like to illustrate this truth with three games I used to play as a child: "Catch me if you can," "Hide and seek," and "Spin the bottle."

I am constantly amazed at how daring we can be when it comes to the ethics of encouragement. We basically say, "I know encouragement is important. But, there are some of my team members that I don't like. There is no way that I will encourage them. But I know it is important not to make a big deal of my favoritism, so I simply will be selective in my encouragement. I will encourage those I like and leave alone those I dislike. And, those I leave alone will never know I am encouraging others and not them."

We blatantly say, "Catch me if you can!" And, we assume that we will not be found out. Nonsense! We will be caught!

It is almost as if that insecure partner has a built-in radar system. The radar system is particularly adept at picking up inconsistencies in employee treatment.

If you have favorites, and the insecure partner is not one of them, the insecure partner will surely find it out. He can catch you, and he will!

Worded another way, we say, "I'm going to hide my encouraging of the other and it will be up to you, the insecure partner, to seek and find instances of favoritism." The insecure partner will welcome the challenge and he will find what you are trying to hide.

Now when this partner has caught us at the point of our favoritism, when he finds what we have unsuccessfully tried to hide, he "spins the bottle" on us. He not only wins, he becomes a poor winner.

He turns the table and begins to play a series of sinister games on us. He makes a big deal out of what he has found. And, once again, the leak leads to a flood of problems for the team and for the manager.

This reaction may be internalized and revealed through withdrawal or excessive pouting or resignation. Or, it may be externalized and manifest through an apparent and open get-even attitude!

Either way, the problem does not have to happen. Remember to be ethical in your encouraging; don't have favorites!

Now, it is much easier for me to write that preceding paragraph than it is for you or me to apply it. "Don't have favorites!"—that's a tough order. Perfection is probably impossible here. It may be impossible to remain unbiased always.

I am simply suggesting that we focus on fairness, that we attempt to be impartial in our encouragement. And, we must remember: if we are going to be unfair, if we are going to be selective, if we insist on having favorites, we will be caught!

Why? Why will we be caught? The encouragement manager who has favorites is unusually transparent.

A Code Of Ethics

There is a code of ethics for the encouragement manager. It basically states: "As a manager of encouragement, I will strive to dispense the Kudzu–killing chemical fairly. I will, to the best of my ability, seek to be unbiased. I will try not to have favorites. But if I do have favorites, if I am indeed unfair, I will expect the consequences."

Now, at this point, I think I know what may be going through your mind. You're thinking, "Some people don't deserve encouragement. I cannot condone this or that, or his or her behavior."

We will, of course, be addressing this dilemma in a later chapter. But for now, let me lift up the differences between management by encouragement and condoning attitudes or behavior.

Management By Encouragement

Management by encouragement is person-centered. This does not mean that it overlooks or disregards ineffective or counter-productive attitudes or behavior. To the contrary, management by encouragement addresses and confronts any opinion or conduct that seriously harms the company, department, staff or classroom.

The manager of encouragement does not cowardly and superficially withdraw from confrontation. The motto for the manager of encouragement is not "pacify at all costs."

The encouragement manager must not look away from the problem. In fact, he must look into the problem and into the person or persons involved. Because management by encouragement is dual focused, it not only emphasizes affirmation of a particular employee's strengths, it also stresses the careful and constructive confrontation of a particular employee's weakness.

Management by encouragement is a unique, systemic and systematic approach to leadership, and it works! But, the encourager must attempt to adhere to a code of ethics.

Try not to have favorites. Remember, if you do, it will leak out. And, don't forget, eventually the leak will lead to a flood of problems.

The Ooze Factor

Because we are such transparent creatures, much about our personhood actually oozes out to the people around us. This is particularly true when it comes to the issue of having favorites.

It is almost as if the insecure partner has raised his antenna. He is particularly sensitive to being second fiddle to other team players. And, if you treat someone else as first fiddle, he will certainly sense it.

Why? It will be sensed because the ooze factor is so powerful. This is to suggest that our attitudes, our opinions, our belief systems, have a way of oozing out from our words and behavior.

We will address the ooze factor later when we suggest that there is a particular contagion involved here. But, for now, remember that attitudes ooze from one person to another person, from one department to another department, from the team to the institution!

The "ooze factor" here is exceptionally powerful. Remember, a manager plus a favorite equals a leak!

CHAPTER 8

Encouragement Plus Enthusiasm Equals Effectiveness

Wednesday, June twentieth, brought the cure!

I had just finished speaking for the Atlanta Business Expo And Conference. I was trying to walk, or navigate, my way from the Inforum, around the Atlanta Apparel Mart, through the Atlanta Merchandise Mart, to the Peachtree Tower. It was an impressive maze.

I finally arrived at the law offices of John R. Harris. John had called me the night before. He mentioned that he had read that I would be speaking in Atlanta that next day and wondered if we could get together for lunch.

It suited me fine; lunch always suits me fine! And, John was actually going to buy.

I've known John Harris for at least four decades. By birth we are cousins; by choice we are friends; by necessity he is one of my lawyers! John is a partner in a patent and copyright law firm.

It had been awhile since I had seen John, but he looked like I expected. He looked like a lawyer. John could always mix stripes and dots and suspenders and end up looking like a lawyer. Today was no exception.

John took me to a nice, quaint restaurant in downtown Atlanta. We ordered our food, and then it happened. John actually paid!

We began to eat. Before I knew it, John's well-hidden agenda surfaced as he said, "Stephen, it's time for the book!"

Encourager—Encourage Thyself

An hour and a half later, we were still talking about "the book," this book. And, John was not charging me a thing, for the meal or for his time. Halfway through the conversation, we returned to his office.

I sensed a sincerity in John Harris that day that I have not yet forgotten. The confidence that young man had in me and "the book" touched me deeply; it also triggered some deep feelings and precious memories within me.

Management By Encouragement

As I sat in John's office, awestruck by his interest and confidence in me, I found myself thinking about John's dad. I don't think I mentioned this to John at the time. He first discovered these thoughts when he read the manuscript.

But on that day, in John's office, I saw so much similarity between John and his father, Judge Robert H. (Bob) Harris.

Bob Harris died many years ago. And, when we lost him, we lost one fine man. When we lost Bob Harris, we lost a maverick of sorts, a gifted lawyer and judge who loved wild flowers, native trout, and doing favors for people.

Judge Robert Harris installed the ceiling in our remodeled basement. He did that as a gift, one of many gifts. I miss Judge Bob Harris; I miss his uniqueness. I miss his encouragement!

Yet, here was his son, encouraging with all the vigor he could muster. The John Harris who sat behind that desk that day and his dad, Judge Robert H. Harris, so much a part of my history, kept running into each other in my mind. It was a very special moment!

John's encouragement about my writing the book came to an end as he said, "Motivator, motivate thyself!"

Of course, I immediately corrected that by saying "Encourager, encourage thyself."

Suffice it to say, John's encouragement that day contributed significantly to the creation of a motivational environment that lead me to push some of my own buttons. I have often asked myself why John had such an impact on me on that day, Wednesday, the twentieth of June.

The same two answers normally surfaced. John had an impact on me that day because he was highly enthusiastic and extremely believable.

Evaluate Your Enthusiasm!

Enthusiasm is contagious! It won't make the decision for another, but it certainly can help provide an encouraging setting. And, when believability meshes with enthusiasm, something powerful takes place!

Many times, I don't even make the airport before I'm studying the evaluations I have received from a just completed keynote or seminar. When the presentation has been deemed unusually effective, I will always notice references to enthusiasm.

And when you are deemed unusually effective as an encouragement manager, I bet it will have something to do with your enthusiasm evaluation! And you do want to be enthusiastic, don't you? But sometimes it just won't come, will it?

When You Want To Sneeze, But Can't

Most of this book is being written in the last half of 1990. At this particular writing, the Southeast United States is scorching. The summer heat is unbelievable. Silver Queen Corn, grass, shrubs, trees are dying! Why even the normally stout Kudzu is showing an occasional droop! We need water!

And, so often, it looks like it is going to rain, but it will not rain. The wind will pick up, the clouds will darken, everything looks perfect for rain. But it does not happen! We get our hopes up and are disappointed.

It makes me think of how I feel when I think I'm going to sneeze. I feel a sneeze coming on; I position my face for a sneeze but it never happens!

Many would-be encouragers feel enthusiasm coming on. It looks like its going to happen; they ready themselves. But, enthusiasm never happens, enthusiasm will not come!

It is just like the rain or the sneeze that looks like it will come but never does!

Enthusiasm Redefined

"I just can't, Mr. Gower," the student said; and she was speaking for many in the speech class. She felt that she could not stand up and speak in public.

Similarly, many managers feel that way about enthusiasm: "I just can't be enthusiastic. I want to, but I cannot!" Much apprehension about enthusiasm is caused by a misunderstanding, or at least a limited view, of enthusiasm.

On that hot afternoon in June, my attorney friend, John Harris, was extremely enthusiastic. John had obviously redefined enthusiasm!

He was not loud; he did not jump up and down; he did not indicate a cheerleading, rah-rah, mentality, but he was extremely enthusiastic!

There was a specific intensity to John's words and behavior. When he encouraged me, he articulated himself with enthusiastic clarity. He had obviously thought about his concern for many months. The very inflection in his voice indicated his enthusiastic support of my book.

He was encouraging me to write the book; his enthusiasm was apparent. But, his enthusiasm was not "apparent," if one's definition of enthusiasm is limited to the normal perception of enthusiastic behavior.

John was quiet, but enthusiastic! He sat in his seat; his excitement was jumping all through his voice! He was not loud but he was forceful! Again, John was enthusiastically encouraging me; he was enthusiastically encouraging me in a most unusual way. *Enthusiasm, redefined enthusiasm, represents encouragement's fourth ingredient.* And, its reminder formula is: *encouragement plus enthusiasm equals effectiveness.*

You Don't Have To Shout

Redefined enthusiasm does not necessitate a jumping up and down. One reason that so many people have so much trouble with this type of enthusiasm is that it is alien to their very nature. They are not jumpers!

I recognize that the differentiation I am trying to make may appear to be somewhat unusual. But, enthusiasm has as much, if not more, to do with the quality of our words and actions as it has to do with the quantity and energy level of our language and behavior. Intensity is not the same thing as volume! Enthusiastic emphasis or affirmation does not have to be limited to a loud cling-clang!

You don't have to change your personality to

be enthusiastic! To the contrary, you remove the camouflage that has hidden your real personality.

For more than a decade, I've worked with business leaders, with law officers, with health care professionals, and with college students who finally found it necessary to redefine enthusiasm. They had earlier found it "impossible" to be enthusiastic. Their discovery of their own enthusiasm had much to do with this crucial new understanding of enthusiasm!

Enthusiasm, or intensity, is not limited to a loud cling-clanging. Enthusiastic behavior does not have to express something you don't feel. To the contrary, enthusiastic behavior, if it is to be effective, must be felt sincerely.

Enthusiasm, or intensity, must communicate a significant and intense feeling or concern for something, or for a particular mission, or toward a particular person. And we must remember, we do not have to yell to communicate this type of enthusiasm. And, we do not have to be who we are not to communicate enthusiasm. Again, however, the problem is: we have learned unusually well how to camouflage our real feelings.

One way we camouflage our intensity is by suggesting that the only way we can be enthusiastic is to yell and rant and rave. That is, for us, awkward, aggravating and self-defeating. We will argue that since we cannot be that way, we cannot be enthusiastic.

We must recognize that enthusiasm is not the implanting of an alien feeling or expression. It is appropriate to suggest, however, that when we display this sort of pseudo enthusiasm, we will alienate others.

No, enthusiasm is not the implantation of an alien attitude and behavior; it is the unleashing of an intensity within. And, this unleashing can certainly be soft-spoken!

He Said Nothing, Yet He Still Said "No!"

He's been gone much more than a quarter of a century. And I still love to call him "Daddy!" I remember asking Daddy if I could take the car out late, real late. He said that I could not. I mistakenly asked a second time. He merely looked at me and did not open his mouth. But that look gave me an unequivocal and extremely enthusiastic second "no!" My father was extremely enthusiastic, very forceful; he didn't say a word. He did not have to; his whole persona was blasting out a forceful "no!"

Now that we are at least thinking about a reorientation toward enthusiasm, particularly as it relates to the integrity of the personality and to the possibility that enthusiasm can indeed be soft-spoken, let me lift up three particular, and perhaps unique, approaches to a redefined enthusiasm for the encouragement manager.

Particularize—Don't Pabulumize

As he seeks to create a motivational environment, the encouragement manager will find it necessary and helpful to affirm enthusiastically the accomplishments of the team members. When this manager of encouragement affirms, he should not dispense "pabulum," he should particularize the affirmation.

To seek to encourage in very generic fashion is almost wasted breath. To encourage at the point of the particularity of the accomplishment is to encourage enthusiastically!

Pabulum may be something with which you are not familiar. Pabulum, however, may be something you were once familiar with, but have not thought about for decades.

Pabulum is a nutritive substance I took as a

child. I am sure that it was very good for me, but I remember very little about its taste.

For our purposes, "pabulum encouragement" is communication that is not remembered very well. And, it is not remembered very well because it is insipid, bland, naive, trite or simplistic. The communication involved with "pabulum encouragement" belongs to that nonspecific, almost plastic, genre of expressions that includes the following: "I enjoyed that." "You did well." "That was a good job."

Certainly the above might be better than nothing at all. But it falls far short of particularized affirmation!

When I use the concept, "Enthusiastic, particularized affirmation," I refer to that family of concrete and direct expressions that include the following:

I appreciated the forcefulness, sincerity and uniqueness of your presentation. I particularly appreciated the fact that you were so familiar with your speech that you found it unnecessary to use notes!

You handled that last customer so well! Sometimes, I am amazed at your particular ability to listen! You seemed extremely natural and patient with that particular customer. You gave her the idea that you had all the time in the world for her. And, I think she picked up on it. She'll be back!

Can I tell why you did such a good job with that project? You did well because you were thorough. You were organized, and to the point. You also did well because you were creative. Why, I don't think anybody else would have thought of using actual interviews in the presentation. You were accessible. I think everybody appreciated how you remained several moments after your presentation to handle questions.

Please note that these above expressions are not enthusiastic because they are spoken loudly, they are enthusiastic because the encouragement manager was wise enough to particularize them. Many team members are familiar with "pabulum encouragement," they are not as familiar with "particularized encouragement." Accordingly, when they are the recipient of "particularized encouragement," they are surprised, and very appreciative.

Don't ever forget, no matter how old we get, we still pay attention to pleasant surprises! And particularized encouragement, in this day, is a pleasant surprise.

We Particularize When We Are Mad

The very interesting and sad fact is that we will remember to particularize when we're mad. When we are upset, or angry, we will be very sure to be specific. When we are frustrated with team members, when we want to confront at the point of weakness, we will use precise, particularized language. We will be certain that they know exactly how we feel.

However, when the issue is strength affirmation, rather than weakness confrontation, we are inclined to be vague, general, bland and nonspecific! When the issue is weakness confrontation, we remember to particularize. But when the issue is strength affirmation, we forget to particularize; that is when we pabulumize!

We are very direct, and at times emotional, when we are confronting an employee at the point of weakness. However, when we are affirming an employee at the point of strength, we are vague, ambiguous, bland and general.

If we are confronting at the point of weakness, we will give the employee, the intended receiver of our message, something to sink his teeth into. If, however, we are affirming at the point of strength, we will not give the intended receiver of our message, the employee, something to sink his teeth into!

It is a matter of emphasis—an inappropriate emphasis! Unfortunately, it is very clear to many employees that, as far as the manager is concerned, weakness confrontation is more important than strength affirmation. In other words, the message many employees receive is this: "Confronting you at the point of your weakness is more important to me than affirming you at the point of your strength!"

What the manager is saying is this: "When it comes to weakness confrontation, I want to be sure you get my message, and accordingly I will particularize. However, when it comes to strength affirmation, I am not as interested in being sure that you get my message, hence I will use pabulumized language."

Is it any wonder then that many employees get the idea that the only thing the manager is interested in doing is complaining? Many insecure partners are wondering if the manager ever notices positive contributions and if the manager is ever willing to applaud those positive contributions.

Perhaps at this point, it is helpful to summarize the double hurt that the manager does to the team. If the manager feels appreciation for team players, he not only has the tendency to assume they know how he feels; when he does affirm the contribution, he also has the tendency to use pabulumized language. In other words, sometimes we simply assume somebody knows how we feel; other times, we express appreciation, but in pabulumized, not particularized, fashion.

The effective manager of encouragement must do better!

Remember, a particularized, affirming surprise equals enthusiasm! An intense feeling of appreciation and affirmation that is expressed in particularized fashion is heard, appreciated and remembered, even if it is soft-spoken. It facilitates the pushing of that "ah-ha" button — "Ah-ha, they really do notice; and they really do care!"

The Perspective Of Distance

When the manager of encouragement is molding a motivational environment, he will find it helpful to intensely affirm achievements of the staff. When he affirms, he may not always find it best to do it immediately! The decision to wait may be the most enthusiastic thing to do.

The training session was over. I was a ball of sweat and as hungry as I could be. I was in a hurry to go across the street because I knew one of the Southeast's finest family-style restaurants was across the street.

But the lady wanted to talk. She said some kind words about the presentation, specifically about this "perspective of distance" concept. And then, she said something I had never heard before. She mentioned that she worked in the area of special education and would often congratulate her young men and women immediately after the accomplishment of a particular feat. And, it would not sink in.

However, if she waited, sometimes as much as two weeks, to articulate her affirmation, it would register. The young student would "get the message."

I knew that approach worked in management by encouragement. I had not pondered its effectiveness in special education.

Remember, many of our team members are insecure partners. And, when we remember what they have done several days or weeks down the road, and then mention it to them, they are, again, surprised. It is as if they are feeling: "You still remember that! Why it's been ten days since that happened. I didn't think it was that big a deal."

But, "the big deal" is that the encouragement manager remembered! And, the insecure partner will remember that the encouragement manager remembered.

Your enthusiastic remembering may catch the insecure partner by surprise in a most positive way.

Again, this is enthusiasm redefined. It is not an alien cling-clanging. Many times, it is not cheerleading mentalities that catch the attention of the insecure partner; it is the perspective of distance that catches his eyes and his ears.

It is interesting to note at this point that if the issue is weakness confrontation, we have no difficulty bringing the point back up a day, a month, a year or even a decade later. If the issue is our anger, we will not forget it and we will not fail to bring it back up again and again. But, if the issue is strength affirmation, we will fail to bless it with the perspective of distance!

Before leaving this point, let me recognize that utilizing the perspective of distance is not always the smartest thing to do. There are two red flags.

Some events are so significant, and some partners so insecure, that enthusiastic affirmation must immediately take place. Also, some of us are so forgetful that we may fail to remember to express affirmation two weeks down the road.

But, there are many occasions when the decision to wait, to utilize this perspective of distance concept, is the most enthusiastic thing to do!

Encouragement managers, at least occasionally, bless your statements of affirmation with the perspective of distance. And, please remember, when you do bring the issue up, be sure to remember to particularize what you say.

It is the experience of many managers of encouragement that this "double whammy" of enthusiasm, that is particularization plus the perspective of distance, will prove to be extremely important in enthusiastically expressing affirmation to insecure partners!

Use The Exclamation Point!

When the encouragement manager is constructing a motivational environment, he will find it beneficial to affirm enthusiastically the behavior of his team when that team performs effectively. As he articulates this affirmation, he will want to conclude his statement, at least occasionally, with an exclamation point.

Management By Encouragement

For several years, I have been very intrigued by, and much involved in, two specific and related issues. These issues are radio versus television and spoken language versus written language.

The penetration of television strongly suggests that it reigns superior over radio because you cannot "see it on the radio." Those of us who appreciate radio will counter that you "can see it on the radio" because of the "mind's eye."

In similar fashion, enthusiasts of written language will argue that its benefits far outweigh those of spoken language. One particular advantage that written language has over spoken language, they will argue, is that you can utilize the structure and emphasis of punctuation in written language. They suggest that the spoken word will not be served by punctuation. They contend that speakers cannot punctuate.

Nonsense! If radio reaches the imagination of the mind's eye, spoken language can reach the eyes and ears of the mind.

Speaker, encourager, don't let anyone tell you that you cannot punctuate when you seek to articulate encouragement. You can! Let me encourage you to use the exclamation point.

You Don't Even Have To Raise Your Voice!

Once we understand the power of inflection, we can begin to encourage enthusiastically through the exclamation point. Inflection is a variation in the tone or pitch of the voice. Inflection does not necessarily mandate a change in volume — the level or variation of sound. Inflection has more to say about how you say something than how loud you say it.

Without significantly varying volume, and by utilizing inflection, one can take almost any sentence and deliver those words in at least three different ways.

Here's the example I use for my students:

(1)   The university of my town has a good football team.

(2)   The university of my town has a good football team!

(3)   The university of my town has a good football team?

As indicated by the written punctuation marks, the same set of words can be spoken in three different styles. This occurs not so much through change in volume as it does through inflection — a variation in tone or pitch.

Management By Encouragement

The first sentence ended in a period. For too many of us, our spoken sentences always end in periods. Many times a period indicates that we have used very little, if any, inflection. Our listeners may be kind when they simply say that we are speaking in monotone. They will use stronger language when they say we sound monotonous. The encouragement manager dilutes his statement of enthusiastic encouragement when he uses nothing but the period to articulate verbally the completion of a statement.

In our example, the second expression reveals an enthusiastic statement. Through the inflection in his voice, the speaker sounds believable. The listener hears and sees the exclamation point. The listener is inclined to believe that the speaker is excited about what he is saying.

Remember, the encouragement manager is transparent. The listener can tell if the speaker is really meaning what he is saying or if the speaker is going-through-the-motion. And, a genuine exclamation point will indicate excitement from the speaker to the listener.

The third expression concludes with a question mark. A question mark can express doubt, deliver sarcasm, or merely reveal a whimsical, teasing attitude. Basically, one should not use the question mark following an enthusiastic statement of encouragement. The dangers inherent here are many. A mixed signal is most certainly received by the listener. The listener will probably not only not feel affirmed, he will most definitely feel put down.

A Caveat—Handle With Care

The exclamation point can be overused. For our purposes, the exclamation point is a powerful aid for the speaker, for the encouragement manager. It helps the encouragement manager emphasize the statement of encouragement. It is effective because it is seldom used in spoken language. If it is overused, its effectiveness is diluted. In other words, any strength taken too far becomes a weakness.

The exclamation point is a powerful tool for the encouragement manager. Be selective when you use it in your written affirmation. Be selective when you utilize it in your spoken affirmation. Handle the exclamation point with care.

And, do not just use the exclamation point when you are mad. Use the exclamation, at least occasionally, when you are glad.

You Cannot Offer What You Do Not Possess

Enthusiasm is a contagion. It is essential to the creation of the motivational environment through management by encouragement. We have suggested that once you redefine enthusiasm, you remove it from the limits of a noisy, cling-clangy environment. You don't have to shout your enthusiasm. You can emphasize it through particularization, distance and the exclamation point.

That is precisely what my lawyer and friend John Harris did on the day he encouraged me about the point of this book. He expressed and emphasized his encouragement, not through a rah-rah cheerleading mentality, but through particularization, distance and the exclamation point.

However you choose to express your enthusiasm, you must have it before you can express it; you cannot effectively express what you do not feel. One reason John Harris was so effective in encouraging me was the fact that he felt what he said.

When it comes to strength affirmation, enthusiastic application of the Kudzu-killing chemical is essential. But, don't apply it, don't say it, if you don't feel it. Similarly, if you do feel it, do say it. And, do say it enthusiastically!

CHAPTER 9

A Focus Plus A Focus Equals Versatility

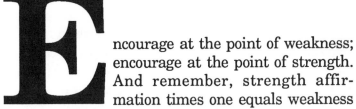ncourage at the point of weakness; encourage at the point of strength. And remember, strength affirmation times one equals weakness confrontation times two. It's two-foci! But, be careful!

Time-release vitamin C brought the remedy. Five intense presentations had been scheduled within a twenty-four hour period. Two days before the start of a series of presentations, I began taking time-release vitamin C. Already feeling somewhat weak in my voice, I had been concerned that my voice might not hold up.

Now, I still don't know whether the vitamin C actually strengthened my voice, or whether I just thought it would and received a corresponding psychological boost. Either way, I managed to deliver all the presentations; my voice was apparently unscathed.

It is my understanding that time-release or control-delivery medicines are made so that the medicine is released, not all at once, but over a period of time. As I understand it, there is a coating process which can make this possible. You take a pill at noon; some medicine is released almost immediately, hours later other medicine is unleashed from that same pill.

The Kudzu-killing chemical is a time-release chemical. It is a two-foci substance. You can control its delivery. You can release management by encouragement when someone has made a significant and positive contribution. You can unleash management by encouragement when someone is having a difficult time, or when you are having to confront at the point of weakness.

In other words, you can control how you can deliver this chemical. You can apply it when you care enough to affirm; you can administer it when you are concerned enough to confront. When the manager of encouragement dispenses this versatile Kudzu-killing chemical, he can choose to focus at the point of strength or at the point of weakness. Management by encouragement is a two-foci chemical. *Awareness of encouragement's two-foci, or time-release nature, is the fifth ingredient of encouragement.* Its reminder formula is: *A focus plus a focus equals versatility.*

This is not a superficial approach! Realistically, management by encouragement does not always take place in an environment that is limited only to strengths. The encouragement manager will have to confront weakness. To suggest the contrary will be both inaccurate and naive.

The thrust of this book deliberately emphasizes the importance of strength affirmation over weakness confrontation. However, to understand the need for strength affirmation and to comprehend the inherent danger in excessive weakness confrontation, we must first analyze our basic preoccupation with weakness.

Why Are We So Weakness Focused?

I often wonder if there really is such a thing as a superiority complex. And, I often suspect that most of us possess, and respond from, an inferiority complex. Perhaps it is our preoccupation with our own weaknesses that helps explain the fact that we dwell on weaknesses. Now, we certainly respond to this common denominator, our preoccupation with our own weaknesses, in very different ways.

Some of us react to our weakness-based focus in a manner that causes other people to perceive us as egotistical, self-centered or arrogant. Others of us respond to our weakness-based focus in ways that lead people to perceive us as timid, shy, back-offish and reluctant. We are simply responding to our weakness-based focus in different fashions.

This weakness-based focus is manifest in a plethora of behavior patterns. It will be helpful to discuss two of the common behavioral responses that evolve out of a weakness-based management or employee style!

Enticement

The enticement response to a weakness-based focus is articulated in this fashion: "I do not feel good about myself. You, however, seem to feel good about yourself. Accordingly, you probably are good. Therefore, if I can get you to say good things about me, if I can entice you to brag on me, I should feel better about myself." Some insecure partners have such a significant weakness-based thrust that they acquiesce control about how they feel about themselves to other people. In reality, these persons are thriving on manipulation, people-pleasing.

Management By Encouragement

It is not the mission of the encouragement manager to fuel these attempts at manipulation. It is, however, helpful for the encouragement manager to understand the power of weakness preoccupation over the insecure partner. Rather than fueling the attempts at manipulation, the manager of encouragement systematically and systemically seeks to create a motivational environment where the insecure partner, or the enticer, desires to contribute legitimately for his own more substantial reasons, and not simply for reasons of people-pleasing. In other words, the encouragement manager seeks to create an environment where the insecure partner begins to establish and respond to his own authentic agenda, rather than the superficial accolades derived from others.

Demoralization

The demoralizer responds to a weakness-based focus in this fashion: "You feel better about yourself than I feel about myself. Therefore if I can make you feel worse, I will in effect be making myself feel better. If I put you down, I will be building myself up!"

If the enticer thrives on manipulation, then the demoralizer thrives on confrontation. This confrontation, this Kudzu, chokes out any real hope for unity and team building.

I mention these two models to suggest how powerful a weakness-based focus can become to the insecure partner and to the team. I choose the terms enticer and demoralizer because, to me, they best describe a person who thrives on manipulation and a person who thrives on confrontation.

It is important for the encouragement manager to understand the power of weaknesses over us all. And when the encouragement manager refuses to respond to the enticer and the demoralizer, the encouragement manager is actually nurturing Kudzu!

The enticer and demoralizer models may help the encourager understand the insecure partner. It is most important that the encouragement manager also understand himself at this point of weakness preoccupation.

It is my experience that one reason managers are so adept at finding another's weaknesses and focusing on those weaknesses is because they are so experienced at discovering and concentrating on their own weaknesses. In other words, the encouragement manager is inclined to confront the weaknesses of others because he has so much experience confronting his own weaknesses.

Now that we have spent some time justifying the intensity and extent of our weakness preoccupation, let us begin to articulate how one can confront weakness when weakness confrontation is indeed in order. Again, to suggest that weaknesses must not be confronted is very naive and inappropriate. There are times when the encouragement manager has to confront at the point of weakness. And, he may have to confront with vigor.

Do It Like A Doughnut

This chapter takes me back several decades. I remember one of my first supervisors. I particularly recall when he asked me to come into his office. At that particular time, I was having rather serious difficulty with some of my fellow workers.

I'll never forget how he began the session. He began it at the point of strength affirmation. I guess I could have expected all sorts of assaults upon me at the point of my weaknesses. He opted, however, to focus initially on my strengths.

As a result, I found that when he was dealing with my weaknesses, I was listening. I was not acting in the defensive fashion in which I was accustomed to act. I was listening! And the reason

I was listening to him while he was confronting me at the point of my weaknesses was that he had initially taken the time to affirm me at the point of my strength. I could listen to this man because I was not totally and utterly threatened by him. And I was not totally and utterly threatened by him because he had affirmed me.

Now this supervisor did not refer to what he did as the doughnut experience. I'm sure that term never entered his mind. But, for a good while now I have turned to the doughnut as a helpful device to illustrate weakness confrontation at its best.

If the hole equals the problem or the weakness being addressed, the doughnut around the hole equals some mode of strength affirmation at the beginning and at the end of the session of confrontation. In other words, when it comes to weakness confrontation, the encouragement manager might want to consider surrounding the confrontation with strength affirmation.

You May Have To Look Hard

Granted, sometimes we struggle to find anything positive at all. In some of our seminars, suggestions for opening affirmation statements in the midst of a confrontation series have been most interesting. They range from "You were only two hours late today, thanks for the improvement," to "At least you buttoned your shirt today."

On a more serious note, the stage for effective weakness confrontation can be set in a less hostile mode if you can find it within your heart and within your mind to begin with some strength affirmation. If retention of your employees is your concern, this approach may be very helpful.

Please, when you are concerned enough to confront, have to confront and do confront—do it like a doughnut!

Let Your Silence Be A Buffer

Now before we move to strength affirmation, the major thrust of this book, let's suggest one particular scenario that often develops in the area of weakness confrontation. I refer to the ranting and raving employee who, in very obnoxious fashion, enters the manager's office.

Weakness confrontation is sure to be addressed! Either the employee's weakness, or the manager's weakness, or perhaps even a third party's weakness will be addressed.

On many occasions, in our seminars, participants vigorously nod their head when we describe a situation where an employee is literally yelling his heart and mind out to the manager. I notice the head nodding increasing when I suggest one, possibly helpful, response to the one who is ranting and raving.

In many instances, the best thing to do here is to do nothing. Worded another way, sometimes the best thing to say here is to say nothing. It is my experience that many times the best weakness confrontation, in a situation like this, is a response on the part of the manager that indicates silence.

When silence is indicated it has a marvelous way of serving as a buffer to the ranting and raving employee deeply involved in an issue of weakness confrontation. There is something about silence that will encourage many insecure partners to self-correct! I am always amazed at the intensity of the audience's head nodding at this particular point in a seminar. It is my understanding that their combined experience validates this silence as a possible, valid option for weakness confrontation!

Strength Affirmation Has Plenty Of Merit On Its Own

We have just finished suggesting that a wise manager may choose to be silent when an employee is confronting and even indicating a weakness. We have also indicated that a manager's strength may be to affirm another at the point of that other's strength in the midst of weakness confrontation. Now, we must strongly suggest that strength affirmation has plenty of merit on its own.

Not only does strength affirmation offer an entrance into serious and helpful weakness confrontation, strength affirmation is appropriate in day-to-day management. Yes, the encouragement manager can affirm his own strength to be silent, in spite of the urge to yell back. The manager can also vastly contribute to the team when he is able to recognize and affirm the strengths of the team members.

- Strength affirmation will help you build your team.
- Strength affirmation will help you keep your best employees.
- Strength affirmation will help you teach your students.
- Strength affirmation will help you keep those students.

- Strength affirmation will help you build relationships.
- Strength affirmation will help you keep those relationships.
- Strength affirmation will enable you to communicate.
- And, strength affirmation will help you continue communicating.

Find And Keep!

One of the nursing home corporations out of the Midwest had decided to come south for a retreat. They had asked me to meet with them and speak for their closing session.

The president of this particular corporation, the very first person I met upon arriving at the retreat site, was a sheer delight. I'll never forget our two-and-a-half hour walk together in the Northwest Georgia mountains the night before the closing seminar. As I walked further and further with this unique man, I increasingly sensed that there was something very special about him. My conversation with his people the next day would support my suspicion.

This gentleman had a tremendous retention rate of top quality people. He surrounded himself with great coworkers; he allowed them to do their job; and he held on to them because he paid attention to them!

Throughout the country, employees are giving up. They will act out their quest for attention through verbiage and through their transparency. They will be ignored. They quit!

If you want employee retention, pay attention! If you want to articulate attention in its finest form, affirm your people at the point of their strengths!

Little Worries, Big Losses!

It was an interesting sight. The massive jet had just landed at the St. Louis, Missouri, airport. We were taxiing to the gate.

Several of us noticed a very tall man beneath us. This man, obviously a member of the ground crew, was covering his ears. Apparently, the sound of the plane was a serious aggravation to him. He had evidently lost his ear plugs!

Those of us on the plane were doing everything we could do to get this man's attention. He was unusually tall. The wing of our plane looked like it was going to hit his head.

The man was so concerned about his ears, he almost very seriously injured his head! Our wing missed him by inches.

So many of the weaknesses we focus on are powerfully petty. Sometimes, we concentrate on them so diligently, that we almost seriously injure our head, our employee!

This Kudzu-killing chemical is one powerful force. It has dual capacity. You can channel it toward weakness confrontation and it will work, if you don't forget the doughnut. You can direct it towards day-to-day strength affirmation and it will allow you to maximize the potential of your team.

However you choose to use it, handle it with care! Don't lose your head trying to protect your ears! Don't lose a quality employee because you have magnified petty weaknesses due to your own preoccupation with weakness.

Strengths And Weaknesses Travel Together

Please, remember this! With every set of strengths, there travels a parallel set of weaknesses. Strengths don't travel alone!

As I work with diverse groups from a broad area, I never cease to be amazed at the point of one particular reality. That reality is this: some of the most gifted people in any organization are also, many times, some of the most eccentric people! In other words, some of the most gifted people I know are also some of the most unusual people I know. The encouragement manager must recognize this reality — that strengths and weaknesses travel together.

If you want an aggressive, outgoing employee, do not automatically expect that he will also be gifted in the area of fine details. If you drastically need an employee who is exceptionally gifted in operations, in orchestrating schedules, events and deadlines, please don't expect that employee also to possess automatically the skills to speak to and train a large staff.

Whatever the weakness-and-strength mixture of your team members, please learn to expect and accept the reality that there will indeed be a mixture within each employee. This expectation should help make your job easier.

If strengths and weaknesses travel together within the employees, then appreciation and tolerance must travel together deep within the manager of encouragement. As much as possible, don't focus on the weakness; concentrate on the strength. Both you and your employee will be glad you did.

Don't misuse the Kudzu-killing chemical. Management by encouragement works well with weaknesses when you "do it like a doughnut," when you surround the weakness confrontation with strength affirmation. It works particularly well with strength affirmation when you apply it in such a way that it will be remembered!

CHAPTER 10

The Trip Equals Detours Plus More Detours

They ought to give you bonus frequent flyer miles for long delays!

It was to be a routine trip from Atlanta to Birmingham. Due to a thunderstorm attack on much of the Southeast earlier in the day, Atlanta's Hartsfield International Airport was experiencing tremendous delays. My particular flight finally departed two and a half hours late. I could have actually driven to Birmingham in the amount of time that I spent waiting.

Nevertheless, in retrospect, I am grateful for that specific delay. It presented me with another fresh reminder of the reality of delays and detours. Once again I was able to observe how different people respond to delays in various ways.

One fellow traveler groaned the whole two and a half hour period. The volume of his groaning intensified as the length of delay increased. Another simply slept. A third spent time working over his briefcase papers. One pouted; one slept; one worked!

The experienced air traveler will learn to anticipate delays. The veteran encouragement manager will grow to the point where he anticipates detours. It is what you do with your delays, how you use your detours, that really matters! *The awareness of the reality of "travelling by detour" is the sixth ingredient in encouragement.* The reminder formula is: *the trip equals detours plus more detours.*

Remember, it is not only what you do during the delay or detour interval that matters; it is also important what your detour or delay experience teaches you. In other words, do you reach the point where you are able to use your "where you have been" productively and profitably?

Twenty-Three Years Of Experience!

The young man was as kind as he could be when he asked if he could speak to me for a moment. He told me that he was wondering when the next public sales seminar would be scheduled. I responded

that it was going to be a long time before we did
another sales seminar in his area. He proceeded to
tell me how very much he needed the seminar and
stated his frustration with his lack of experience.

At that point, I suggested that we sit down
right there in the restaurant and talk one to one for
just a few minutes. The young man, certainly without
knowing it, had touched one of my buttons.

I asked the young man how old he was. He
replied that he was twenty-three years old. Our conversation immediately took off.

Experience Redefined

"Well that means you have twenty-three years
experience," I suggested.

He replied, "What do you mean?"

Then, I continued in a fashion somewhat similar to this:

You have twenty-three years of
experience of studying and failing to
study; you should remember how you
felt each time you received your grade.
You have twenty-three years of forgiving and getting even; you should remember the price you paid for revenge

and the dividend you received for forgiving. You have twenty-three years of ignoring and listening; you should remember the different feelings your various behavioral responses caused you to have. You have twenty-three years of experience in putting other people down and building other people up. You have traveled on the main highway, and you have traveled by detour. You probably have learned much from each experience. By now, you should certainly be able to compare what works for you to what works against you!

In life, and in management by encouragement, we travel by detour. Our "where we have been" can inform our reactions. Our "where we have been" can torture us, or it can tutor us!

The wise manager of encouragement will not only recognize the reality of traveling by detour, he will also profit from the detour experiences. He will encourage his team members to expect detours and to learn to profit from their detour experiences.

It Can Be Tough

One can be more than forty-nine thousand!

I was on route to Des Moines, Iowa. Within moments, I had struck up a conversation with the young man seated next to me on the plane.

I asked "Where's your home young man?"

He replied that he was from a small town in North Carolina. I remember the name of that town well. And, I remember equally well his name. I will never forget either.

The gentlemen was headed to Manhattan, Kansas. He was one of forty-nine thousand reservists who had, at that time, been activated because of the Middle-East situation. He mentioned he was leaving behind a wife, a one-year-old, a two-year-old, and a sales career.

On that flight, I discovered how the intimacy of a one-on-one conversation, or relationship, can be much more powerful than a much larger figure representing a removed and distant phenomenon.

Forty-nine thousand reservists had been called up for duty. That, in and of itself, was very significant. To see and encounter the frustration of one of them, eye to eye, was even more disturbing, and somewhat unnerving.

Awkwardly, I'm sure, I sought to comfort the young reservist. Almost impulsively I referred to a book I mention quite frequently in the presentations.

Dr. M. Scott Peck's *The Road Less Traveled* begins in an interesting fashion. Dr. Peck introduces the first chapter on discipline with the words "Life is Difficult." Dr. Peck goes on to share that once we recognize this great truth, it no longer has the same type of power over us.

As we struggled with the reality of detours some thirty thousand feet up in the sky, we became close, even though we were together for less than an hour. Dr. Peck's thought from *The Road Less Traveled* seemed to help that young, frightened reservist from the Tar Heel State.

The same concept is certainly one to be recognized by the manager of encouragement. Encouragement managers will confront many detours.

Past mistakes will surface. The encouragement manager can allow those experiences from his distant past to haunt him, or he can allow them to help him.

In the present, the manager of encouragement will experience both the detours that he brings on himself and the delays brought by others. The wise encouragement manager will learn from these detours rather than allow them to strangle away a gusto for the project, snuff out appreciation for the team members and choke away affirmation of his own value.

The effective manager of encouragement will not nurture the Kudzu that detours might present; he will kill the Kudzu by controlling, and perhaps even benefiting from, the detour experience. Also, in the daily administration and team building efforts, the manager of encouragement will be presented many opportunities to enable the team members to travel by detour.

Remember, the encouragement manager is transparent. When he effectively responds to detours, team members see it. When detours pull the upper hand and dwarf the encouragement manager to little more than "a reactor," team members see it.

Not only by example, but also by direct confrontation of the issue, the encouragement manager can enable the team member to accept the reality of detours and learn, as best one can, from those detours.

How Come You Don't Have Any Lumps On Your Arms?

As a young parent and uncle, I used to wrestle with all the "very young ones" during our family reunions. I would never win, but would always try to justify the outcome of the match with "but you had me out-numbered."

One day, I was badly beaten. I happened to be wearing one of those unusual T-shirts. It did not have half sleeves; it was not cut off at the shoulders; all it had was two thin straps holding the body of the shirt over the shoulders.

Now this type of undershirt is, as far as I am concerned, very ugly, particularly if you are not blessed with an imposing physique. I believe that there is one redeeming trait of this type undershirt. It is great for staking tomato plants.

Well there I am, exposed in this ugly undershirt. Again, I am losing the "rough house" battle with all the children. And, then he says it! Almost, out of the blue, he says it!

"How come you don't have any lumps on your arms?"

The young boy totally baffled me until I remembered what he had been doing earlier in the day. He had been watching wrestling on television. And, all the big, muscular wrestlers had lumps, or bulging biceps on their arms.

Well, I do too now! I was embarrassed and took up a weight lifting program.

The young man's comment gave me an opportunity to talk to him about lumps. I shared three thoughts.

First, I told him that we are all blessed with lumps, or skills, or talents. If we build those lumps, they will grow; if we neglect them, they will dwarf. I reminded him that we should always remember who gave us these lumps, these talents.

Next, I suggested to him that there was a second type of lump. It was the lump we received when we made mistakes and bumped our heads against the wall. It was the bruise, or lump, we received when we ran into an object, or perhaps someone else, like The World Champion of Wrestling. The important thing to remember, I told him, was that we could learn from these lumps, these mistakes, these detours.

Finally, I described to this young man a third type of lump. I suggested that it was the lump you sometimes feel deep in your throat. You feel as if you are swallowing a golf ball. And you say, "Goodness, I am being used right here, right now!"

Naturally, the "lump reality" expressed in this part of the book relates to the second type of lump — that bump on our head caused by that mistake, or someone else's mistake, or simply through the fault of no one. This lump illustrates the reality of traveling by detour. Its very presence reminds us that we can learn from "our where we have been."

The encouragement manager must fully comprehend this reality, both in himself and in the team members. We all travel by detour!

To ignore this reality, or to respond inappropriately, is to nurture Kudzu. However, to recognize and effectively utilize these detours, or lumps, or experiences, is to take a significant step towards the killing of Kudzu!

Specifically, the manager of encouragement will: anticipate detours, accept their reality, analyze them lump by lump, apply what is learned from the analysis, and perhaps occasionally, actually appreciate the experience.

Anticipate

Expect them, they will come. When you are trying to encourage, you will encounter this lump, the detour.

It was the most significant thing my first significant employer gave to me. I had worked for him before, but on this occasion I was now in sales.

Things were going unusually well. I was breaking record after record. Indeed, I was the beneficiary of beginner's luck.

On one particular day, my boss asked to speak to me. I had no idea what was coming, but sensed a seriousness in his voice, and on his face.

"What you're doing in sales here is almost unbelievable. Your sales record keeps building and building and I am very proud of you," he said.

"But," he added, "I want you to know that I know it will not always be like this. Your sales cannot always go straight up. There will be peaks and valleys. When a valley comes, and it will come, I will be just as proud of you."

What a gift he gave me! What a reality he had recognized! He was not programming me for failure; he was positioning me for a meaningful and productive journey.

Just as a salesman will encounter declines, detours, on his trip to the top of the sales chart, so will the encouragement manager experience peaks and valleys as he seeks to encourage his team and kill Kudzu. Just as a salesman is freed when his employer indicates a comprehension of the fact that there will naturally be some declines, so will the manager be released from an unrealistic expectation when he reminds himself that detours in the encouragement process will come.

On that day, my boss was very kind to tell me that it would all right if I could not keep up my initial pace. I do remember him as an unusually kind man.

He was also very smart to tell me that he expected detours, or temporary declines. I imagine in the long run I was much more useful to him, and much more pleasant to the other team players, because of his conversation with me. I do remember him as a very smart man. It was exceptionally smart of him to tell me it would be all right to slip some. Certainly, this will not work with everyone, but it worked with me. It will work for the encouragement manager.

Yes, the encouragement manager should anticipate detours in the encouragement process. He should expect declines in the killing of Kudzu. In the long run, this anticipation will prove mutually beneficial to the encouragement manager and to the team! It will take pressure off both!

Accept

It's one thing to be able to anticipate detour experiences. What do you do when they happen? You try to accept them!

This does not mean you like them. It does not mean that you agree with what their occurring says. It simply means that you try to accept the reality of the presence of the detour.

It is as if you are saying, "This is the way it now is. Now, what do I do?"

The effective encouragement manager will not reject the reality of the detour; he will not seek to "blame it away" on someone else. He will accept that this is "the way it now is."

He will accept the presence of the decline that, at least temporarily, replaces the ascent. He will accept the reality that something discouraging has happened that temporarily has reversed the cycle of encouragement. He will accept the existence of the fact that something has happened to the team that, at least temporarily, means that team destruction has replaced team construction. He will accept the fact that, at least temporarily, Kudzu–killing has been replaced by Kudzu nurturing!

After the encouragement manager consistently confirms that "this is the way it now is," he then asks, "now what do I do?" And, what he does is this: he analyzes!

Analyze

I had just made a terrible mistake! I had purchased a muscle shirt, a tank top shirt. I had rationalized that such a shirt would be most comfortable for jogging. I was in the bedroom, preparing to place the top over my naked tank when one of the young ones entered the room.

In a state of apparent disbelief, he blurted out, "There's something about that shirt that does not go with your body!"

He was correct. Indeed, there was everything about that shirt that did not go with my body!

A muscle shirt is designed to allow for, and exhibit, powerful and well-defined muscles. I had none to exhibit.

And the only thing that became well-defined, when I put on the tank top or muscle shirt, was my potbelly. The shirt that had been created to show off bulging biceps was showcasing my stomach. It took all the stretch the shirt had in it to allow room for the tummy.

Once the encouragement manager accepts the detour, accepts the fact "this is the way it now is," he then explores "now what do I do?" What he does is this: he analyzes!

Management By Encouragement

The manager of encouragement recognizes or accepts, that "there is something about the muscle shirt that does not go with my body." Worded another way, "there is something about this detour that does not go with what I'm trying to accomplish, or to encourage here."

He then moves from acceptance to analysis. Acceptance is not the back door; it is the front door. Acceptance is not a last step; it is the first step, following anticipation. Acceptance merely introduces analysis.

The encouragement manager, seeking to kill Kudzu, analyzes the detour by asking precisely, "what is there about the shirt that does not go with my body; specifically, what about this detour conflicts with what I'm trying to accomplish, or to encourage here?" The encouragement manager paints a picture in his mind of the detour experience and analyzes precisely what most bothers him about the detour.

After he comprehends precisely, or particularizes, what it is that bothers him about the detour, he begins to analyze why the detour happened. He specifically seeks to understand why the shirt does not fit, or why it happened. He moves from asking "what it is wrong" to exploring "why it is wrong."

At this point, it must be noted that the word "wrong" is helpful. It should also be noted that the manager of encouragement may later choose to reexamine the use of that word.

Nevertheless, there is an analysis of the detour. If something is to be corrected, something must first be diagnosed, or analyzed. In other words, if something is to be adjusted, one must first understand what needs to be adjusted. And to make an adjustment, an adjustment that does not always have to be remade, the encouragement manager must seek to understand not only what needs to be realigned, but why a realignment is necessary.

Not only must he ask what about the shirt does not fit, what about the detour conflicts with his long range goals, he must seek to figure why the shirt does not fit, why the detour happened. He explores what caused the detour. He diagnoses!

To restate, the diagnosis, or the analysis, is two-foci. The encouragement manager not only seeks to understand what needs to be adjusted; he also explores why an adjustment is necessary, or what happened to cause the necessity for the adjustment. Worded another way, the manager of encouragement analyzes the detour so that, in the final analysis, the detour experience will, at least to some degree, prove to be meaningful.

The wise encouragement manager, determined never to allow Kudzu the upper hand, always seeks to learn from traveling by detour. This learning process will necessitate a thorough analysis, or diagnosis, of the detour.

It must be added here that the learning process, this analysis, may even prompt an unusual discovery. It is quite possible that the encouragement manager had earlier always dreaded detours. A thorough analysis of the detour may leave the manager to readdress, or rethink that dread. In other words, if he learns enough from the detour, he may in retrospect look upon it not with dread, but with respect, and perhaps even with appreciation.

Detours do not have to torture the encouragement manager; detours can tutor the encouragement manager. The issue of appreciation of the detour will be addressed later in this chapter. For now, remember—the great tutorial position is the position of analysis!

Apply

The young man was giving his first speech in Speech 105. I had been looking forward to his presentation, since he had been a unique member of the class. He was very popular with the classmates. I too had found myself drawn to his personality, particularly his dry wit.

He was strong, stately looking, almost exemplified some sort of heroic aura. He possessed what I like to refer to as a positive presence.

At this moment I cannot remember the topic of that first speech, but I certainly remember him standing there. That moment has lodged permanently in the catalog of my mind!

He began his speech in adequate fashion. Soon, I noticed him stumble in a very minor way. Within seconds, he stopped. He probably spoke for less than a minute. The speech was to be a minimum of three minutes in length.

I looked up from my note pad. I was seated close to the speaker's podium and could easily observe the transparency of his personhood at that moment.

He was taut; the positive presence he had earlier exhibited had been dwarfed. Each member of the class could feel and observe an awkward tension between the strength of his presence and the utter weakness or frustration he exhibited in that moment.

Within a matter of seconds, I noticed myself hurting with him. His eyes were swollen with tears. He would be able to catch them and choke them off. No one but me would notice.

"I cannot finish," he said.

"Well why don't you just sit down and give your speech to me later," I suggested.

He was most appreciative. He presented his speech later with very little difficulty. He learned enough from that experience, and the many conversations we had about that experience, to deliver his next speech in the front of the class. When I think about all my students, now spanning more than a decade, this young man comes to the front of my mind.

He had anticipated what might happen; he accepted what did occur! He analyzed and applied what he discovered.

He ultimately received a very satisfactory grade. And I imagine that he learned more about himself, more about detours, and more about growth than he learned about speaking in public. I would also like to think that he learned something about the power of encouragement.

For more than a decade now, I have sought to teach my students and our seminar participants that there is a tremendous common denominator that binds all people who speak in public. That point of commonality is nervous energy. It is my experience that nervous energy is a reality for all of us who speak in public.

Hundreds of students and seminar participants have mistakenly labeled the challenge for the speaker in relationship to this common denominator, this nervous energy. They have suspected that the goal for the speaker is to eradicate or eliminate nervous energy.

I strongly suggest that those who strive to eliminate nervous energy will fail. The elimination of nervous energy for the speaker is an unreachable goal. It is my conviction that nervous energy will always be present for the speaker. This is true even for, and perhaps particularly for, the veteran public speaker!

For you see, the challenge in response to the common denominator of nervous energy is not elimination; it is utilization. It is not eradication; it is redirection.

The effective public speaker learns to channel nervous energy. He learns how to make it work for him rather than against him. He learns how to apply nervous energy as a plus rather than a minus, as a blessing rather than a curse.

Through intense preparation and many other specific skills, the effective public speaker learns to direct nervous energy in such a way that nervous energy can actually become an advantage. The wise public speaker learns how to apply nervous energy effectively to his advantage. He redistributes nervous energy. He channels nervous energy so it ends up working for him rather than against him.

Likewise, the prudent encouragement manager discovers that he can redistribute the detour. He can apply what he learned from the detour in such a way that the detour actually becomes a plus, not a minus.

The goal for the manager of encouragement is not the elimination of every possible detour. Detours happen! The goal for the encouragement manager is to learn how to channel traveling by detour in such a way that detours help growth and the encouragement effort rather than hurt growth and the encouragement effort.

The analysis of the detour experienced in encouragement is of no power if what is learned is not applied. And the aggravation of the detour does not have to be the last word if the encouragement manager has the whole thing turned around in such a way that the detour actually ends up working for the team rather than against the team, for encouragement rather than against encouragement.

It's the attitude that matters. Is the detour viewed in such a way that it intimidates or controls the manager? Or, is the detour viewed is such a way that the manager is the one who takes charge?

If the manager of encouragement is successful in reigning superior over the negative, destructive power of the detour, if the manager is able to channel the detour in a positive way, the manager and the team will benefit! This power struggle between the detour and the manager does not take place in private.

For you see, the team is always watching the manager. Again, the manager is very transparent at the point of the detour. Therefore, if the manager is able to channel the detour experience advantageously, to apply what he has learned to his benefit, then the team members will get the idea that they can do the same thing.

Management by encouragement through example is perhaps no more powerful than it is at the point of traveling by detour. The encouragement manager can maximize, indeed multiply, his efforts when it becomes obvious to him and to the team members that he has been able to apply effectively what has been learned from the analysis of the detour.

Remember, apply what you learn from your own and others' mistakes. Your resiliency during the detour experience, the very fact that you are courageous and wise enough to learn from it, will be mutually beneficial for you and your team!

Perhaps the most encouraging thing you can do for your team is to anticipate, accept, analyze, and apply your own detour experiences to the point that you grow. The team will observe your transparency and will thus be encouraged to follow suit!

Appreciate

Perhaps they don't call them detours, perhaps they refer to them as failures or breakdowns or sidetracks or mistakes or "my bads." However they label them, many of the very effective managers of encouragement with whom I have worked have suggested, either directly or indirectly, that their most significant points of growth have come through traveling by detour.

In other words, these encouragement managers would contribute a significant portion of the credit for their growth to detours. They find that interesting and surprising because they had been programmed for decades to dread the detour. Now the dread actually has become a deep source of personal and team growth. In retrospect, they now appreciate what they used to dread!

As you seek to kill Kudzu, to create motivational environments through management by encouragement, please remember that detours happen. Anticipate them! Accept the reality of their occurring. Analyze the detour experience. Apply what you learn. And, perhaps for you, the dread will occasionally be replaced by appreciation — appreciation for what has been learned by traveling by detour!

CHAPTER 11

Paying Attention Equals Retention

ash behind your ears."

"Do your homework."

"Don't beat your sister!"

"Stephen, you can't see the forest for the trees."

I grew up bombarded by the parental verbiage hurled the way of many children. However, the dictum that has most permanently lodged itself in my mind is, "You can't see the forest for the trees."

When my parents felt compelled to issue these words, they were, of course, calling into question my capacity to perceive reality. I choose to borrow and modify their words for the purpose of addressing an attitude that has weakened the holding power and effectiveness of many organizations.

This attitude is directly related to the inordinate and shortsighted emphasis that many managers inappropriately place on the destination. In effect, this phraseology seeks to call into question our capacity to perceive reality as it relates to the development of human resources.

They Cannot See And Enjoy The Journey For The Destination!

Enough! We have saturated our team members with a goal or destination emphasis. To the detriment of the team, and to the detriment of productivity, many managers have become entirely too destination-focused.

The error here, of course, is not in having goals that serve as obtainable and meaningful objectives. The managerial mistake is to so overstate these goals that the importance of the journey experience is underestimated, if not ignored.

Yes, A Strength Pushed Too Far Can Develop Into A Weakness

It has occurred hundreds of times as I have observed college students and business professionals strive to improve their public speaking skills. An agenda for improvement will be suggested and the speaker will move from one extreme to the other.

The speaker would initially indicate no familiarity with the content of a speech; weeks later some improvement would occur; much later the speaker would deliver the speech in a memorized, detached and very impersonal manner. Lack of familiarity was addressed. The familiarity level improved. A weakness had actually become a strength. But now, it had been taken too far. The speaker had become so familiar with the speech that the speech sounded lifeless, memorized, canned and almost farcical.

Another speaker initially had no eye contact with the intended receivers of the message. There was improvement. Again, a weakness became a strength. The strength was taken too far and the speaker would actually "stare down" some members of the audience.

A third speaker presented a speech in monotone fashion. There was no variance in the pitch of the voice. The issue was addressed. The student made significant progress. A weakness actually becomes a strength. The speaker had discovered the power of inflection. But later, the strength is taken too far. A pleasant, natural inflection was replaced by a forced, rhythmic, choppy, robotic, mechanical "sing-song."

From subject familiarity to eye contact to voice inflection, a strength was pushed too far and developed into a weakness!

Unfortunately, like these speakers, many managers have taken an obvious weakness, developed it into a strength and then pushed the strength too far, back into a weakness! A classic example for consideration for the encouragement manager is the issue of goals, or the subject of the destination.

Certainly in the distant history of many organizations, and perhaps even in the recent history of some, one will discover an aimlessness or purpose-lessness that literally haunted the company, the association, the community, the church, the individual. Something was missing!

Someone recognized the vacuum and gave the organization, or the individual, the structure or the gift of goals and destinations. A curative for the rudderlessness was prescribed. The prescription became the focus. The focus became goals and more goals.

Organizations began to zero in on this focus. Event-focused organizations would retreat again and again to their endless quiver of goal-arrows! One target was selected; one target was hit; and another goal-arrow was drawn!

It all seemed to work—for awhile. Somewhere along the way of the arrow something went wrong. A strength was pushed too far and it developed into a weakness. The destination, the event, the goal became the only thing that mattered.

It was pushed so much that the team member was denied seeing or enjoying the journey. The staff could not enjoy the journey because of the exaggerated emphasis on the destination. To compound it all, once one destination, or goal, was reached, another was quickly targeted.

The bombardment of exaggerated goal or destination emphasis played havoc on the diverse landscape. It was almost as if some of the arrows missed the target, the goal. Some arrows veered away and seemed to hit right at the heart of the team. The hit hurt!

It hurt productivity; it hurt predictability; it hurt people. It caused a problem. The problem became retention. People were acting out their frustration, discouraging one another, and quitting.

Somewhere along the way of the arrow, management had forgotten to pay attention to the journey. How unfortunate! For, had they paid more attention to the journey, more bull's-eyes could have been actually scored!

The servicing of this journey experience is the seventh ingredient of encouragement! Its reminder formula is: *paying attention equals retention.*

To The Quiver Of Goal-Arrows Add A Satchel Of Journey-Delights!

The effective manager of encouragement does not just carry a quiver of goal-arrows. He also totes a satchel of journey-delights. The successful encouragement manager pays attention to the journey. He services the journey! He well recognizes that paying attention equals retention.

Service must be perceived as an active verb, not a complacent noun. If we want our employees to actively service our customers, our clients, our patients, then we must actively service our employees. If our desire is for the customer, client, patient to appreciate the journey experience with us, then we must actually pay attention to the journey experience of our employees, our team members.

It is the resurfacing of the "ooze" factor. What we put into our employees is what will ooze out to the customers, the clients, the students, the patients.

But how do you service the employee? How do you pay attention to his journey experience? How do you add a journey delight? You just simply bring along a L-O-L-L-I-P-O-P! You listen, observe, log, label, investigate, ponder, obligate and process!

Listen

First off, you listen. The employee, particularly the significantly insecure partner, will articulate concerns. In the first analysis he may not expect you to act on them at all, but he will expect you to listen, to pay attention.

Not only do you listen to the concerns, you also listen out for the accomplishments. Listen for what is bothering him, and listen for what he is doing well!

Observe

And remember, the insecure partner will not always act out his frustration or need for attention verbally! Accordingly, you will have to listen to more than his words. You will need to pay attention to, or service, his transparency.

This particular part of the book is being rough-drafted on a Delta jet. Less than two hours ago, I completed a presentation for a large hospital in the Southeast. Just prior to my leaving, one of the participants asked to chat for a moment. One could replay his scenario a thousand times. Earlier that day, he experienced an extremely frustrating two-hour session with another member of the staff. He explained that he could just not understand why she was acting in such a fashion. He explained the situation and recounted that it didn't make any sense!

When I suggested that all of her behavior might be a plea for his attention, he initially acted surprised. His hurried mental perusal of that idea seemed to indicate that he was willing to explore that possibility.

Listen to the team members. Listen to their words. Observe their transparency!

Remember that many insecure partners may not possess the inclination nor the courage to ask verbally for your attention. This does not mean that they do not desire it. And it certainly does not mean that they are asking for it. It merely means that they might not be asking for it verbally. But there are many ways insecure partners will cry out and act out their appetite for your attention to their concerns and accomplishments. Observe!

Log

After listening and observing, log for yourself the concerns and the accomplishments of the insecure partner in question. Put them in writing. List them in the order of their importance, not as you perceive their importance to be, but in the order of importance that you think the insecure partner would have written them down.

This logging serves several purposes. It ensures that you focus on the concern, or perhaps even the accomplishment. The very fact that you list them helps you to remember them. Once they are written down, you naturally can refer to them later.

Finally, by logging the concern or accomplishment, you are able to relate to the insecure partner that you took them seriously enough to go to the trouble of writing them down. You validate the fact that you recognize that they had concerns or had made accomplishments.

It is possible that you may not want to share this log with them. It is also likely that you may choose to share it with them. It will be good to have it if you ever need it to indicate your level of seriousness in relationship to their concerns and their accomplishments.

Label

The next step in this servicing process, this paying attention to the journey, the L-O-L-L-I-P-O-P, is to label the different entries in the log.

There will be two categories. One category will be in the area of the insecure partner's concerns. The other section will be related to the insecure partner's accomplishments. Now, you have some direction and focus as you seek to develop some plan of particularized attention for the concern and for the accomplishment.

Investigate

Now, you investigate. You may need to pursue one or possibly two tracks.

Your first investigative pursuit would be in the area of concerns of the insecure partner. Remember, most of your partners are just that — insecure!

If you have not heard or observed any specific concerns, then no investigation on your part is necessary. If, however there are concerns, then you go back and investigate to discover the facts. Of course, you always keep in mind that the insecure partner's perception is, to him, perhaps more important than the facts. A thorough comprehension of the facts behind the concerns will help you develop your response.

Your second track of investigation is in the area of the insecure partner's accomplishments. The more you learn about his accomplishments, the better you are positioned to effectively pay attention to the accomplishments.

It is extremely important to understand and implement this point! The more thoroughly you investigate the accomplishment, the more effectively you will be able to service the need for attention and to particularize your affirmation!

Yes, a thorough investigation of the accomplishment will enable you to particularize precisely why you appreciate the accomplishment and the team member. The lack of investigation of the particulars leading to and shaping the accomplishment will result in "pabulum." To particularize through an investigation of the accomplishment is to bring a special delight to the insecure partner's journey.

The investigation positions the encouragement manager for a response. It is a very crucial stage in the L-O-L-L-I-P-O-P process. It must follow your listening, observing, logging, and labeling. It must precede, or inform, the remaining steps of the servicing of the journey!

Ponder

One is naturally inclined to make observations about the concern or accomplishment as soon as one hears or observes the concern or the accomplishment. This pre-investigation observation is natural, but must not be final. The post-investigation observation is crucial to the legitimate servicing of the journey!

After the facts and perceptions are in, the encouragement manager ponders. Worded another way, he ruminates.

In the mountains of Northeast Georgia a lot of ruminating takes place. It occurs when a cow chews the cud. Technically, the cud is the part of the food that leaves the cow's first stomach and reenters the mouth. There, it receives another chewing!

To ruminate is to chew again. Just like the cow ruminates, the effective encouragement manager chews again the concern and the accomplishment.

This second chewing occurs after the investigation. Here, the manager of encouragement thoroughly considers the facts and the perceptions. He carefully ponders what happened and why it happened. This dual pondering, "the what and the why," applies to both the concern and the accomplishment.

Management By Encouragement

Perhaps here is the appropriate place to note that the insecure partner's main concern may well be that his accomplishment may not have been noticed. Nevertheless, whatever the concern and whatever the accomplishment, the effective encouragement manager will ponder what the investigation has revealed.

Obligate

Here, the prudent manager of encouragement makes a decision. He may decide to do nothing. Or, he may decide to do several things. At this point, he obligates himself.

It is helpful to note that the encouragement manager obligates himself to do something. This is not the point where he obligates himself to the insecure partner in a specific and concrete way. It is, however, the place where the encouragement manager obligates, or commits, himself to a specific course of action.

The manager may decide to drop the whole issue. He may deliberately choose to postpone any action. Naturally, he will want to weigh all possible consequences to these first two options. Even if he chooses to drop the issue or postpone any specific action, he chooses to articulate to himself what is to be done.

Quite probably, the effective encouragement manager will decide to make a specific response. The purpose of this step in the process is to ensure the clarity of a commitment to a particular action that needs to be taken.

Here the encouragement manager obligates himself to that commitment. Again, this is an internal pledge. The encouragement manager binds himself to follow-through with a course of action that is a response to what he has heard, observed, logged, labeled, investigated, and pondered.

Now, with this obligation, with this personal commitment, the encouragement manager is positioned for the final step of the L-O-L-L-I-P-O-P treat. Armed with this internal mandate, the manager of encouragement is now bound and determined to follow-through. He is ready to process what he has obligated himself to do. He makes a promise to himself; and he keeps it. He processes the promise!

Process

If, for our purposes, the word service resembles more closely the active verb rather than a complacent noun, then the same is true here for the word process. The effective encouragement manager proceeds to process what he has obligated himself to do. He implements his program of response. He handles the nuts and bolts of the obligation. He does what he said he would do. He processes the promise.

If he has decided to address a particular concern or accomplishment in a certain fashion, he carries it out. The listening, observing, logging, labeling, investigating, pondering, and obligating has suggested a particularized action! Now, the encouragement manager acts.

He processes any recognitions, realignments, responses, promotions or changes that must take place. He does it, or sees to it that it is done!

This final stage caps off the L-O-L-L-I-P-O-P treat for the employee's journey experience. Remember the L-O-L-L-I-P-O-P: listen, observe, log, label, investigate, ponder, obligate and process your responses to the concern, to the accomplishment.

Trust the L-O-L-L-I-P-O-P

Don't make this more complicated than it is. Allow the simple structure of the L-O-L-L-I-P-O-P to help you add a journey-delight to the experience of your team members.

If the L-O-L-L-I-P-O-P does nothing more

than cause you to listen and observe, to log and to label, to investigate and to ponder, and to obligate and process, then it will aid both you and your team members. If all the L-O-L-L-I-P-O-P does is to force you to bring attention to the need for particularized attention, then that is a step forward.

Please take the L-O-L-L-I-P-O-P seriously. Use it consistently and effectively. Trust it. It will last a long time. Indeed, it will work for you throughout the journey.

Trust the L-O-L-L-I-P-O-P experience to help lead you away from the poison of assumption and toward the power of particularization! Pay attention to the L-O-L-L-I-P-O-P; it will equal retention!

Remember, service is a verb!

CHAPTER 12

One Equals A Lonely Number

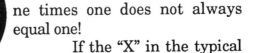ne times one does not always equal one!

If the "X" in the typical multiplication equation is used to illustrate a negative tension, or the reality that one team member is working against another team member, then one times one can equal minus two! In other words, when one team member is literally functioning against another team member, as far as the team is concerned, the team loses the optimum productivity of both team members.

Of course, when two team members are working together, then our "X" indicates a sum of plus two. The team actually benefits from the services of two cooperating members.

The urgent factor for the encouragement manager to ponder is the reality that minus two and plus two equals a difference of four. Worded another way, two team members working against each other do not merely contribute to a minus two factor, they deprive the team of a plus two factor. Accordingly, the team is weakened by a factor of four.

Awareness of the importance of the team is the eighth ingredient of encouragement! The reminder formula is: *one equals a lonely number.* Many times the encouragement manager must significantly experience this doubly damaging team tension before a turn around can become possible.

Bottom-Up!

I was to speak to an association the next morning and had arrived in Houston the night before. The taxi ride from the airport to the hotel revealed a tremendous "Houston at night" scene. I wanted to see more.

The hotel had one of those oscillating restaurants at the top of the roof. My room was on the twenty-eighth floor, not far from the top. I called the front desk and asked how I could get to the restaurant at the top. The clerk told me that I would have to come all the way down to the main lobby and take a special elevator up.

"You mean," I said, "I've got to come to the bottom before I can go to the top?"

"Yes," he said with a most understanding chuckle.

Sometimes, the Kudzu of team tension needs to worsen significantly before the potential manager of encouragement decides to do something. Often, it has been my experience that a team will hit bottom, before it goes to the top! The sooner the manager of encouragement recognizes the destructive power of significant team tension, the sooner he can begin to implement a program of encouragement.

This particular strategy of management by encouragement affirms recognition of a state of disintegration as a first step toward the revitalization and building of the team. To repeat, sometimes you have to go to the bottom before you can go to the top.

The journey towards the top of "teamanship" begins with an awareness of how much we need each other. This particular trek must be taken on a two way street!

Help Me!

It was many years ago. It is as fresh in my mind as if it occurred this morning.

"Help me!"

All else would stop. When you hear those words from a very little girl, you stop what you are doing. You listen and you try to respond.

I had been working on a speech. This little one was playing at the bottom of a huge hill behind the house. She could not get back up the hill. She called for me; she called for an awkward and "very poorly coordinated me."

As has been stated, our seminar participants are often reminded that strengths and weaknesses travel together. Accordingly, appreciation and tolerance must, to a degree, travel together. That little girl knew I had some gifts; she also knew I had a lot of weaknesses, particularly at the point of coordination.

My family has affirmed me at the point of my strengths. They have tried to tolerate my many weaknesses, particularly my inability to navigate myself.

Even as a toddler, so many years ago, that little girl knew I would always be "stumbling towards something." She suspected I probably would literally stumble my way down the hill toward her. She would be right!

It has been that way for decades. It was the

case right after my father died. I was eighteen years old at the time. Then, and ever since then, my mother has been asking my younger sister to cut the trees down on the property.

It certainly was true at Fort Bragg, North Carolina. I was there for a ROTC camp experience. It was awful! The whole scenario was completely alien to a skinny, insecure, poorly coordinated young man.

The only highlight to that experience occurred at five in the morning about three weeks into the camp. The captain was inspecting us. He came to me, glanced at my face and said some most encouraging words.

"Mr. Gower, you forgot to shave!"

I had not shaved for three weeks. He finally noticed. I was on cloud nine!

Approximately three weeks later, the captain would call me into his office. It was evaluation time. If my memory serves me correctly, fifty of us would be accepted for status that would eventually culminate in our being commissioned officers. The others would not pass.

"Mr. Gower, you are number forty-nine."

"I made it?"

"Yes, and I want to tell you why. Perhaps some day the army will need a talker!"

I knew what he meant. We had just finished our last company get-together and they had asked me to speak. It must have been at least tolerable. The captain went on to suggest that perhaps a limited gift of speaking might one day benefit the army.

"Yes, you passed. But, I'm going to put on your permanent record, 'please never put a gun in this man's hand!'"

Coordination has never been one of my strong suits. Many years ago that little girl recognized that reality when she completed her instructions by saying, "Help me, don't fall, don't fall."

Help Me, Don't Fall

The effective encouragement manager sends a dual message to his team members. This message is fundamentally important to the team. It is: "Help me, don't fall."

Oddly enough, for many, the greatest difficulty is in uttering the first part. When it comes to teamanship, it is often difficult to ask for help. For, implied in the asking is the indication that one is willing to receive. Many of us had rather give than receive.

Management By Encouragement

This may surprise you. It is my genuine experience that many managers find it much easier to give than to receive.

I am well aware that this may run counter to the idea that it is always more blessed to give than to receive. However, upon analysis, this actually may exhibit a very high form of giving. To receive from an insecure partner may be the most giving thing one could do.

The prudent manager of encouragement is able to ask for help, and receive help, particularly if that help comes in the form of a unique gesture, or perhaps even in the shape of a compliment. When the encouragement manager receives the gifts of the team members, he is enhancing the team.

We are intentionally choosing to emphasize the power of this phenomenon as we near the conclusion of this book. Many managers underestimate the power of receiving help, unique contributions, and yes even compliments. It is very important to understand that one of the most encouraging things the team leader can do is to receive from the team members.

This reception can have a validating effect on the one giving. Many of the most gifted managers I have ever observed are almost brilliant at this point.

They have learned that appropriately asking for, and receiving help, can significantly contribute to team building and to the encouragement process. This reception can aid tremendously in the development of subordinates.

Rejection can be very discouraging and downright destructive; reception can be both uplifting and encouraging. Whether you ask for help, and then consider changing your mind, or whether the offer of help comes without your invitation, think very carefully before you say, "No." Of course, many times "No" will become essential! But, think first.

And remember, when you say "Yes," when you receive help, you will be contributing to the phenomenon that explains why one times one can equal plus two. For you see, when you receive, you not only validate the giver, you validate receiving.

In other words, when you, the manager of encouragement, receive, you set the example for your team members. Your team members might well respond, "If the successful and wise leader is able to receive, maybe I would be smart to do likewise."

Represented here is a shift from the excessively competitive, and extremely turf-protective, mentality that explains how one times one can equal minus two. This idea runs counter to the attitude that pits overly independent, almost arrogant, team members against each other.

The very idea of receiving connotes an openness that is helpful between the team leader and team members and between the various team members. Remove this capacity to receive one from the other and you create an environment that will become insular rather than team-oriented. In such an environment of isolation, one times one will never be able to equal plus two!

In this instance, the team very much resembles the individual. For just as one individual grows when that individual is open to, or receives, from another, so will the team's performance improve when one member is open to, or receives, from another.

Perhaps enough has been said here. Excessive language can certainly dilute the reality of a particular concept. Suffice it to say that tremendous team-building power surfaces when the encouragement manager is wise enough to ask for and receive help.

And when team members follow suit, when they ask for and receive help, the phenomenon is multiplied! Kudzu is killed, not nurtured. One times one equals plus two time and again.

But to ask for and to receive help is only a first step in this team building process. Now comes the power behind "don't fall."

Not only will the astute manager of encouragement ask for help, he will also articulate to the team member a concern for his well being! If the front end of the team-building concern here is to receive, then the back end is to value. Yes, here too, value is a verb.

Value Is A Verb!

To the manager of encouragement, each team member is not only a source for help, he is also a person to be valued. We not only want someone to help us up the hill, we do not want them to fall in the process.

We service their journey, we pay attention to their steps, particularly as they descend a steep hill. In a variety of ways, we communicate that they matter to us. Surprise of surprises, when they are on the receiving end of our concern, they are actually encouraged to exhibit legitimate concern for each other.

Entering my mind right now is a particular health care facility. Before I was to speak to their management staff, one of their key human resource development and training coordinators spent some special time talking to me. There, she restated to me that her hospital shunned the use of the term "customer" and preferred to use other phraseology.

She explained that her hospital sought not to use the term customer or patient, but terms like "friends" or "visitors." They interpreted these terms in such a broad and inclusive fashion that they not only included patients and patients' families, but managers and employees as well.

It was certainly not the first time I had encountered an organization that preferred not to use terms like customer or client or patient. It was, however, refreshing to discover such a broad and all-inclusive interpretation of the concept.

But it certainly made sense. If encouragement managers could treat their team members as friends or visitors, and if team members could treat each other as friends or visitors, if they could take steps to communicate concern that the other not fall, one times one would be equaling plus two time and again. One has a tendency to be much more gentle with friends and visitors, even if they are fellow team members!

When team tension is building, and team destruction approaching, one times one is equaling minus two. Kudzu is being nurtured.

When team members are receiving from and valuing each other, when team construction is taking place, one times one is equaling plus two. Kudzu is being killed.

Before another one comes into the equation, one equals a very lonely number. One needs another one!

But one does not need that other one to interact in such a way that each becomes less than one. One needs that other one to react with him in such a way that is mutually beneficial. When each one is willing to receive from and value the other one, team building occurs!

Encouragement manager, remember — value is a verb!

Part Three

The Fiction

CHAPTER 13

Fiction: You Can Give What You Do Not Have!

(You Cannot!)

Certainly, in the long run, one cannot incessantly give what he does not have. I frequently remind my students and seminar participants that what one puts in is what will come out.

If they do not put any thought and preparation into their speech or project, then it comes out as a thoughtless mumbo-jumbo. Similarly, if the encouragement manager is repeatedly putting discouragement into his own mind, then that is what will come out - discouragement.

Constantly put yourself down and you will find little reserves to enable you to build up or encourage your team members. Be harsh with yourself; harshness will come out toward others! Look for the worst in yourself; out will come a tendency to view others through the lens of their worst!

Incessantly focus on your own weakness, out will come a weakness-based focus toward others. Expect too much of yourself, out will come unrealistic expectations of your team members. Program abrasiveness in, abrasiveness will come out. Program tolerance in, tolerance will come out.

Be Gentle With Yourself

As an encouragement manager, you are a composite of your choices. What you choose to do and what you choose not to do, the associates you choose and the associates you do not choose, help form the fabric of your management scheme.

The way you choose to treat yourself significantly contributes to this composite, this collage. If you choose to discourage yourself time and time again, that will eventually help shape a composite of team discouragement. If however, you choose to be more gentle toward yourself, that will significantly contribute toward a collage of team encouragement.

Just as team members will not be able to exist in a vacuum, neither will you. Just as there is no neutral territory for the team members, there is none for you. Your team members are either feeding the encouragement cycle, or they are fueling the discouragement cycle. And you, yes you, you are fueling the encouragement cycle, or you are feeding the discouragement cycle.

If you keep browbeating yourself, the issue will no longer be in doubt. For in choosing to discourage yourself, you will actually be deciding to discourage your team members. Kudzu will thrive!

However, if you opt to be more gentle with yourself, you may find yourself more gentle toward your team members. And don't be surprised if you notice encouragement thriving!

Yes, what you put in is what will come out. Repeatedly discourage yourself, out will come discouragement. Constantly encourage yourself, out will come encouragement.

The way we treat ourselves will often indicate how we will treat our team members. Value yourself; chances are you will value your team members. Devalue yourself; you will probably notice that you are devaluing your team members.

Earlier we examined the reality that strengths and weaknesses will travel together in our team members. We suggested that some weaknesses are a very natural extension of some strengths, that there is a corresponding backside to the frontside, a weakness that relates to the strength.

Take for example the strength of sensitivity. You may have a particular team member that is very warm, compassionate and understanding toward the customer, the visitor, the friend. You appreciate that sensitivity toward others. However, when you have to confront this particular employee in a very difficult situation, you may be surprised if he is unusually sensitive toward you as you are confronting him.

Sensitivity is not something our employees can turn on and off very easily. If we are going to appreciate their sensitivity toward others, we will need to be much more tolerant when they are unusually sensitive toward us when we are confronting them. The manager who recognizes that one cannot turn the source of the strength on or off so that the backside never shows will be making a significant step in management by encouragement.

The problem we are seeking to address here, however, is not the difficulty the encouragement manager experiences when he forgets that strengths and weaknesses travel together within the team member. The challenge we are suggesting here is for the manager of encouragement to recognize and accept the fact that strengths and weaknesses will sojourn within him, or within her, the encouragement manager!

Encouragement manager, it is essential that you service your own journey experience. Pay attention to your need for attention. Pamper yourself; be gentle with yourself.

Encourager, be sure to encourage yourself gently!

It's A Difficult Discipline

The concluding part of this chapter is being scripted aboard a Delta jet. I have just finished speaking to a group of health care managers.

Near the conclusion of this particular seminar, I asked the participants to articulate how they felt when negative stress, or distress, was ruling over them. I also asked them to express how they felt when positive stress, or eustress, was their experience. I asked them to verbalize in very specific terms what they did to provide themselves with positive stress experiences.

I had earlier suggested to them that stress was very much like cholesterol. In other words, just as there are good and bad types of cholesterol, so are there positive and negative stress experiences. Just as many of us wrongly assume cholesterol is "all bad," many employees incorrectly assume that stress is "all bad."

I'm amazed at the ease with which these health care managers were able to articulate how they felt when they were experiencing negative stress. I was intrigued, if not appalled, at their difficulty in verbalizing how they felt when they were going through positive stress experiences.

When we entered the time in the session when they were to share their positive stress experiences, to tell what they did for themselves that they enjoyed, I soon understood why they were not able to describe how they felt during their positive stress experiences. They could not describe them, because in very many cases, there was nothing to describe.

It was sad! They were not taking care of themselves. Most of their experiences, in their own perception, were negative stress experiences. I suspect that explains why they were having tremendous difficulty with their fellow employees, resulting in a significant amount of additional stress. Had these health care managers blessed themselves with positive stress experiences, they would have been much more effective managers of encouragement. What you put in, is what will come out!

Program nothing but negative stress, out will come negative stress. Pamper yourself, provide yourself with positive stress experiences for yourself; out will come positive stress! Encouragement manager, take care of yourself. Watch out for yourself. Pay attention to your need for attention—your need for positive stress. Discipline yourself to provide care to yourself.

Encourager, encourage yourself with your own positive stress experiences!

Loose Endlessness?

Before moving to our final chapter, let us quickly address one particular way in which the encouragement manager can nurture himself, rather than Kudzu. This is a very specific device that will enable you to fuel your own encouragement cycle, rather than feed your own discouragement cycle.

One massive gift you can present to yourself is to accept the presence of loose ends. "Loose endlessness" is an illusion.

Structure your thinking so as to allow for loose ends. Just as detours happen, loose ends will also occur. Those of us with the obsession to fix everything, to tie everything together neatly and tightly, must understand that there will always be loose ends. To accept this reality is to take a step toward being gentle with one's self.

Encouragement manager, treat yourself in such a way that the negative stress associated with an exaggerated emphasis on the elimination of loose ends will not overpower you. Accepting the ongoing reality of some loose ends along the way of encouragement will help free you from the potentially destructive consequences of an obsession with loose ends!

Don't focus excessively on these loose ends. Emphasize the growth, the accomplishments. Don't always concentrate on what is dangling or broken. There will always be a hair out of place, a blemish on the skin, a dusty spot somewhere on the newly washed car, some discouraging event taking place somewhere. Look toward the encouraging news.

With at least one eye on encouraging developments, not nagging loose ends, the encouragement manager will notice the inclination to be more gentle with himself. Remember, when you program gentleness in, out will come more gentleness!

CHAPTER 14

Fiction: Kudzu Is Stronger Than Encouragement

(It Is Not!)

Kudzu does not have to win!

When you enter the ring with Kudzu, you can win, or you can lose. But there will never be a draw. Remember, there is no neutral territory. Discouragement reigns or encouragement rules.

If you entered unprepared, you will lose. If, however, you enter the ring as a skilled manager of encouragement, you can win!

As I write this final chapter, my mind rolls back, more than three decades, to my early teen years. I'm reflecting on my monthly excitement when a certain teen magazine oriented toward the outdoors would arrive.

I would devour many of those great articles. I

do not remember any of them now. The ideas to help teenagers earn extra money were very helpful. Except for that vague recollection about that Christmas card company that helped me earn Christmas shopping money, I do not recall any other specific ideas to help adolescents earn extra spending money.

What I do remember about that magazine are the two pictures that would entice me to read about special physical exercises or programs!

The first picture would feature a scrawny, skinny and underdeveloped teenage boy, one with whom I would always identify. The second photograph would involve that same teenager, after he had participated in the special physical exercise program. This second snapshot would reveal the same teenager now revealing a much more muscular physique.

To me, the essence behind the intrigue of those pictures were the words that capsuled or headlined each photograph. Above the first photograph would be the word "Before;" centered above the second picture would be the word "After." The central idea here was that the way you physically appeared before embarking on this new physical fitness program would be significantly inferior to the way you looked after participating in this specific body building technique.

Management By Encouragement

I do not recall that I ever transcended the "Before" stage. But I do recollect that I, apparently along with hundreds of thousands of other teenage boys, would fantasize that "maybe one day I will look like that." It never happened!

Enter the ring against Kudzu unarmed, without any of the skills essential for the effective encouragement manager, and you will resemble that scrawny adolescent before he took steps to build those biceps. Kudzu will batter you, nick your spirit with vicious uppercuts, beat away you breath. If Kudzu does not score a knock out, you may become so discouraged that you choose to give up, to throw in the towel.

However, if you approach your skirmish with Kudzu as a trained, prepared manager of encouragement, you will have Kudzu positioned against the ropes throughout the bout. Your conditioning will have yielded dividends of a victory. You will have performed in a fashion that resembled the teenager after he embarked on his body building program.

The way you produce and lead before you seek to behave like an encouragement manager will vastly differ from your performance after you take serious steps toward management through encouragement. You, and your team members, will be repelled by the

"Before," and drawn to the "After."

Prior to your entering the ring against Kudzu, and as we begin to bring our time together to a conclusion, allow me to share some last minute reminders, some ring savvy suggestions! If encouragement is to indeed out-punch pesky Kudzu, if encouragement is to utilize its strength advantage over Kudzu, then this pre-fight or corner-talk may prove to be a most helpful restatement.

So, to borrow a term from the world of automobile racing, let's seek to avoid "brain fade." If "brain fade" is interpreted as a tendency to lose the power of concentration, let's "brain rush." As we rush to focus our brains on the reality that encouragement is stronger than Kudzu, let us concentrate on, or begin to restate, a few of the concepts that will contribute to the superiority of encouragement against Kudzu. Just as encouragement is stronger than Kudzu, there are other parallel truths relating to strengths that need to be readdressed prior to your entering the ring. So let's begin our capsuling, our quick "brain rush."

Please remember that the journey is stronger than the destination! As important as a goal oriented destination emphasis is, particularly for purposes of focus and productivity, the servicing of the journey will eventually prove to be even more crucial.

Accordingly, in addition to your quiver of goal-arrows, always carry a satchel of journey-delights. And remember to be sure to place in that satchel the L-O-L-L-I-P-O-P: listen, observe, log, label, investigate, ponder, obligate and process your particularized responses to the team member's journey concerns and accomplishments.

You will also want to recall that strength affirmation can be stronger and much more beneficial than incessant weakness confrontation. When you repeatedly refer to a team member's weaknesses, and seldom suggest that you have noticed strengths within the same person, you are fueling the discouragement cycle! When you enthusiastically pay particular attention to that team member's strengths, you will be fueling the encouragement cycle.

You will also want to recollect that the poison of current of consciousness and the reality of transparency are stronger concepts than you think! Your urge to assume that someone knows what you know, what you wish they knew, or how you feel is a very powerful urge. Similarly, the reality of your transparency and your team member's transparency is so potent that it can actually validate or contradict verbal signals.

Finally, don't forget that particularization is stronger than pabulumization! Specific language overpowers general language. The encouragement manager must constantly be aware of the urge to particularize at the point of weaknesses and pabulumize at the point of strengths. Accordingly, this manager of encouragement must make a conscious effort to increase and intensify particularization at the point of strength affirmation.

"Hello" Comes Easier Than "Good-Bye!"

For years it has been my custom to suggest to seminar participants that an opening "hello" comes much easier for me than a parting "good-bye." This has been particularly true during our more lengthy seminars and conferences.

In similar fashion, as it relates to this book, I have found it much easier to begin our time together than to conclude this final chapter. Certainly both you and I have invested energy in that very unique relationship between writer and reader, between sender and receiver. For me there is much more struggle in the farewell than in the initial greeting. The signs indicate it's time to go.

Management By Encouragement

A preponderance of *The Art of Killing Kudzu* has been written at our local library. The personnel are extremely friendly and cooperative at this particular library. When it comes to the hours of operation, particularly the closing time, they have very strict instructions to close promptly. They manage to pull this off with tremendous accuracy.

I have been intrigued with their exceptionally successful system of reminding those still in the library that closing time is rapidly approaching. They use no public address microphone, no loud speakers, no megaphone. The librarian does not quietly tip-toe through the bookshelf and study areas reminding those studying or browsing that it is time to leave.

As a matter of fact, nothing is said at all. However, about ten minutes before closing time, the librarian simply dims the lights. Approximately five minutes later, the lighting is reduced even more. At closing time, the lights are cut off completely. Surprise of surprises, come closing time no one is left reading in the library.

A few minutes ago, we began dimming the lights of this book. Now, it's almost time to turn the lights off. But, before we do, before we say good-bye, please allow me to remind you that Kudzu is destructive and that encouragement is constructive.

Kudzu Is Destructive

Kudzu thrives in an arena where current of consciousness communication is not only tolerated, but passively supported. Kudzu feeds on the manager's assumption that the team members know what he knows, what he wishes they knew, how he feels.

This same Kudzu benefits when the team manager allows his transparency to contradict his verbal signals. Form minus force is allowed to equal farce.

The situation is aggravated when the manager chooses to be selective at the point of encouragement. Kudzu seizes this opportunity. The fact that the manager has favorites leaks out to the other team members; the leak leads to a flood of problems for the manager and for the team.

Further complications set in when the manager pabulumizes at the point of strength affirmation, yet particularizes in the area of weakness confrontation. Kudzu smiles and recognizes this as an exaggerated emphasis on weakness confrontation by the manager. Kudzu grows well here.

This incessant attention to the employees' weakness and obvious rejection of the employees' strengths nurtures Kudzu. Kudzu rejoices that the manager has failed to recognize the two-foci nature of encouragement.

Kudzu then greets the manager's inappropriate response to the reality of detours as an opportunity to score extra points. Kudzu sneers with victory every time the manager refuses to utilize or profit from traveling by detour.

And the manager's preoccupation with the destination and rejection of the importance of the journey grants Kudzu another occasion for pride. Kudzu cannot believe that the manager continues to refuse to service the journey experience of the team member.

What literally blows Kudzu's mind, and brings on Kudzu's most ecstatic reaction, is the fact that the manager still wears blinders that keep the manager from seeing how much the team members need the manager and each other. Kudzu will frolic endlessly when Kudzu is nurtured in this fashion.

Encouragement Is Constructive

Encouragement thrives in an environment where current of consciousness communication is not tolerated. It rejoices every time a feeling is translated into an active response. Encouragement never forgets that a hoot minus a hooter equals hootlessness, that a hoot plus a hooter equals hootfulness. Encouragement always seeks to remember that a care minus a carer equals carelessness, that a care plus a carer equals carefulness. Accordingly, the manager of encouragement is very careful to translate feelings of strength affirmation into deliberate attention.

This same encouragement matures further when the team manager recognizes the reality of his transparency. There is integrity in the relationship between verbal and non-verbal. Actions will validate, not contradict, words. Form will be supported by force. Thus form plus force will never equal a farce. The manager of encouragement will look like he sounds!

And the encouragement manager will constructively contribute to the team member's encouragement when that manager seeks not to have favorites! The effective manager of encouragement will attempt to do this. Perfection need not necessarily be the goal. But awareness of the tendency to have favorites is the goal. The smart encouragement manager will be wise enough to recognize this: if he has favorites, it will be inevitable that the fact will leak out and lead to a flood of problems. The manager of encouragement does well when he seeks to administer the Kudzu-killing chemical, management by encouragement, in an ethical and fair fashion.

Encouragement begins to approach a high point of effectiveness when the encouragement manager has the wisdom and courage to redefine enthusiasm. Encouragement does not allow enthusiasm to be restrained by a definition that limits enthusiasm to a cheerleading "rah - rah" mentality. The prudent encouragement manager will redefine enthusiasm. This manager of encouragement will seek to make strength affirmation much more an issue in the scheme of management. Accordingly, when the manager of encouragement affirms at the point of strength, he will do it well. He will do it with a redefined enthusiasm. He will particularize not pabulumize; he will consider blessing the statement of strength affirmation with a perspective of distance, and he will enthusiastically emphasize his affirming statement with an exclamation point!

The success rate of the manager of encouragement will improve in direct relationship to the manager's appreciation and application of the two-foci, versatile nature of encouragement. Encouragement will prosper when the manager recognizes that strengths and weaknesses always travel together.

Accordingly, the management stratagem must be one of appreciation and tolerance. Certainly, this manager will need occasionally to confront a particular concern or weakness in a very direct fashion. However, this manager of encouragement will be very careful to give the same degree of intensity and particularization to strength affirmation. Worded another way, the encouragement manager will strive to pay as much attention to particularized strength affirmation as he pays to particularized weakness confrontation. When this manager recognizes the dual or versatile nature of encouragement both at the point of weakness and at the point of strength, he will be journeying down the road that leads to the fueling of the encouragement cycle.

There will be detours from that road. The prudent manager of encouragement will nurture his encouragement potential when he seeks to anticipate detours, accept their reality, analyze what can be learned from the detours, apply that knowledge and perhaps eventually appreciate the knowledge that has been garnered by traveling by detour.

Additionally, encouragement will begin to flourish when the manager recognizes the team stagnation that develops with an exaggerated emphasis on the destination at the expense of the journey. The alert manager of encouragement will supplement the quiver of goal-arrows with a satchel of journey-delights. This manager will pay attention to the concerns and accomplishments of the team members. Included in the satchel of journey delights will be the L-O-L-L-I-P-O-P: listen, observe, log, label, investigate, ponder, obligate, process. Yes, this encouragement will further grow when the manager remembers that service is a verb. The manager will pay attention to the journey experience of the team members; the manager of encouragement will service their journey.

Finally, encouragement prospers when there is recognition, indeed celebration, of the team itself. The leader of encouragement seeks to create an environment that encourages one times one to equal plus two, not minus two. This encouragement leader strives to develop an environment that fosters a "Help me, don't fall" attitude on the part of each team member.

When they enter the ring, Kudzu versus Encouragement, Encouragement's constructive character will literally overpower Kudzu's destructive demeanor!

THE ART OF KILLING KUDZU

You Are The Field Marshal

Our time together began with a description of a particular field, my garden spot. You will recall that Kudzu was taking over that field.

Don't allow Kudzu to overpower your field, your team. Remember, you are in charge; you are the marshal of the field, you are the marshal of the team.

What do you see when you look at that field? Is the discouragement cycle obvious? Or, is the encouragement cycle apparent? Is Kudzu thriving? Or, is the place bouncing with encouragement?

I hope that, if you do not now see encouragement on that field, you can at least begin to visualize encouragement bouncing. If you need a reminder about the "bounce power" of encouragement, may I suggest you buy a box of BOUNCE®.

For years, in seminars and keynotes, I have referred to that very special Proctor and Gamble product, BOUNCE. I wish I had possessed a box of that stuff when I was in college. I would have avoided those ugly laundry scenes where, when I was trying to pull apart my clinging socks, the hair on my head would stand on end.

I now know about BOUNCE. One day I found myself reading my BOUNCE box. This is what it said: "BOUNCE's special ingredients are released by the dryer's warmth and tumbling action to make your clothes soft and fresh smelling with no static cling."

Initiate a thorough and consistent application of encouragement on your field. And, get ready for some wonderful bouncing. Chances are that you and your team will be able to apply warmth to those tumbling events that will inevitably occur. What will you then see?

You should notice less harshness, more softness; you should observe less staleness, more freshness; you and your team will not have to cling to the Kudzu static of the past.

Yes, you are the field marshal. You are the general in charge. You can nurture Kudzu; you can fuel the discouragement cycle. Or, you can see that the Kudzu-killing chemical, management by encouragement, is applied; you can feed the encouragement cycle.

It's your call! But, if you don't call for Encouragement, Kudzu will surely call upon you.

Well, it's almost time for the librarian to cut the lights off. I can now say good-bye.

But remember—Kudzu is bad stuff; Encouragement is good stuff; Management by Encouragement can kill Kudzu!

Notes

Chapter 5
- The thought on behavior is found in Paul Hersey, <u>The Situational Leader</u>. New York: Warner Books, Inc., 1984.

- The survey on "Why Customers Quit" was taken from Michael LeBoeuf, <u>How to Win Customers and Keep Them for Life</u>. New York: G.P. Putnam's Sons, 1987.

Chapter 8
- Helpful reading in the area of the use of language can be found in the textbook that I use in my speech classes: Robert C. Jeffrey and Owen Peterson, <u>Speech—A Basic Text</u>. New York: Harper and Row, 1989.

Chapter 10
- The insight into the difficulty of life is found in M. Scott Peck, <u>The Road Less Travelled</u>. New York: Simon and Schuster, 1978

Chapter 12
- I imagine there might be several programs similar to the one I referred to in this chapter. This particular plan, Guest Relations, is currently in operation at Childrens Hospital of Alabama.

Chapter 13
- Helpful reading in the area of positive and negative stress is found in Peter G. Hanson, <u>The Joy of Stress</u>. Kansas City. Andrews and McMeel, 1988.

Chapter 14
- The BOUNCE® description was taken from a box of BOUNCE®, made in the U.S.A. by Proctor and Gamble, Cincinnati, Ohio. BOUNCE® is a trademark of Proctor & Gamble, Cincinnati, Ohio.

Recommended Reading

Bennis, Warren, and Nanus, Burt. Leaders. New York: Harper and Row, 1985.

Blanchard, Kenneth, and Johnson, Spencer. The One Minute Manager. New York: Berkley Books, 1984.

Bramson, Robert M., Ph.D. Coping With Difficult People. New York: Anchor Press/Doubleday, 1981.

Covey, Stephen R. The Seven Habits of Highly Effective People. New York: Simon and Schuster, 1989.

Hanson, Peter G. The Joy of Stress. Kansas City: Andrews and McMeel, 1988.

Hawken, Paul. Growing A Business. New York: Simon and Schuster, 1987.

Hersey, Paul Dr. The Situational Leader. New York: Warner Communications, 1984.

Huseman, Richard C., and Hatfield, John D. Managing The Equity Factor . . . or "After All I've Done For You . .". Boston: Hougton Mifflin, 1989.

Johnson, Spencer. The Precious Present. New York: Doubleday and Company, 1984.

THE ART OF KILLING KUDZU

Kami, Michael J. Trigger Points. New York: McGraw-Hill, 1988.

LeBoeuf, Michael. How to Win Customers and Keep Them for Life. New York: G.P. Putnam's Sons, 1987.

McCormack, Mark H. What They Don't Teach You At Harvard Business School. New York: Bantam Books, 1984.

Nanus, Burt. The Leaders Edge. Chicago: Contemporary Books, 1989.

Peck, Scott. The Road Less Travelled. New York: Simon and Schuster, 1972.

Seibert, Donald. The Ethical Executive. New York: Simon and Schuster, 1984.

Von Oech, Roger. A Kick In The Seat Of The Pants. New York: Harper and Row Publishers, 1986.

Von Oech, Roger, Ph. D. A Whack On The Side Of The Head. New York: Warner Books, 1983.

Williams, Mary. The Velveteen Rabbit. Philadelphia: Running Press, 1984.

Additional Recommended Reading
With A Special Orientation Toward Future Trends

The encouragement manager's demeanor and decisions will be positively influenced by an awareness of future trends. Accordingly, this brief, additional recommended reading list targeted toward those trends, should prove to be helpful.

Cetron, Marvin and Davies, Owen. American Renaissance: Our Life At The Turn Of The Twenty-First Century. New York: St. Martin's Press, 1989.

Corbin, Carolyn. Strategies 2000. Austin: Eakin Press, 1986.

Drucker, Peter F. The New Realities. New York: Harper & Row, 1989.

Gerber, Jerry and Wolf, Janet and Klores, Walter. Lifetrends. New York: Macmillan, 1989.

Naisbitt, John and Aberdeen, Patricia. Megatrends 2000. New York: William Morrow and Company, 1990.

About the Author

Stephen M. Gower is recognized across the nation as a specialist in management by encouragement and in the development of communication skills for leadership! His power-packed presentations have impacted audiences across the country. As founding president of The Gower Group, Inc., Stephen Gower has sculpted a human resource development company that is widely respected for high-energy keynote speeches and professional and unusually effective seminars.

As a professional speaker, Stephen Gower is uniquely appreciated for his explosive enthusiasm and his compelling content! This rare blend of intensity and substance has led hundreds of organizations to invite him to speak. Many associations, corporations, schools and communities have invited him back again and again.

Mr. Gower holds a bachelor's degree from Mercer University and a master's degree from Emory University. He has served, or is serving, on numerous state and regional boards, and is a member of the National Speakers Association. For more than a decade, he has taught public speaking on the college level.

THE ART OF KILLING KUDZU

Throughout the country, Mr. Gower is considered a pioneer in management by encouragement. His keynote speeches and seminars have helped thousands of people discover the unique discipline that is essential for the encouragement manager.

The Gower Group, Inc.
P.O. Box 714
Toccoa, Georgia 30577
1-800-242-7404